ORACLE OF CLARION

THE GODDESS UNVEILED

a story to awaken the heart of humanity

Written by Paula Peterson - Produced by Jerry Drobesh

© 1996 - All rights reserved

THE ORACLE OF CLARION
UNVEILING THE GODDESS
a story to awaken the heart of humanity

Paula Peterson

Published by:

RAINBOW PYRAMID PUBLISHERS
P.O. Box 2437
Fair Oaks, CA 95628 USA
Owner: Jerry Drobesh

This book is a fictional story created from volumes of transcripts of numerous meetings that occurred between the author, the publisher and an extraordinary visitor.

Requests for permission to reprint, reproduce, etc., to:

EARTHCODE & INNER LIGHT NETWORK
P.O. Box 766
Fair Oaks, CA 95628 USA

Spiritual/Personal Growth/Inspirational/Adventure

Cover Design: Lightbourne Images of Ashland, OR
Printed and Bound: Griffin Printing of Sacramento, CA
Editing: Lightworks! of Ashland, OR

Library of Congress: 96-69716
ISBN 0-9653235-0-1

Special Acknowledgments

A universe of gratitude and appreciation goes to Jerry Drobesh, founder of Rainbow Pyramid Publishers of Sacramento who made The Oracle of Clarion possible. Through his faith in the higher power and wisdom that inspired the creation of this story, an idea was born and nurtured through numerous challenges. The transformational power of Spirit was evident throughout the adversities of delays, frustrations and major setbacks as well the rewards of beautiful spiritual revelations and joys.

I thank Jerry deeply for his enduring support of The Oracle, for sticking it out over the long haul and having the perserverance and courage to see it through to completion, even though there were formidable forces against the outcome. It became a project that strained our friendship at times, as if Spirit was testing the strength of our faith with the powerful spiritual truths that weave themselves consistently throughout the story. Indeed, The Oracle of Clarion has proven to be a powerful catalyst for change. May the fruits of our friendship be as a gift to the world and the potential it brings to raise the consciousness of humanity and awaken the hearts of all.

The Author

I dedicate this book, for my part, to my recently departed sister, Karyl, whose love and encouragement helped open the door to my Spiritual awakening and whose presence is still with me. To Paula, my love and deep appreciation to an extraordinary teacher, friend, veil remover, and the inspiration for my contribution to this deeply enlightening book. May the world become a better place because of your love, dedication, and God given gifts, represented in this book.

A special thanks to my wife, children, sister Bobbie, and many friends for the "small joys" that make life meaningful. And to the greatest inspiration in my life, my Mother. You "Lived" the life of "Love" and set the example - and I shall always be grateful - to the "Angel in Disguise"!

The Publisher

Other Acknowledgments

Many important friends and professionals gave generously of their time, moral support and expertise to the creation of The Oracle. It is difficult to mention everyone, and deepest apologies to those who feel they were forgotten. However, those who contributed above and beyond expectations are acknowledged first of all.

Deep appreciation goes to Rich Castro, whose unfailing and supportive friendship over the years has become like a priceless gem. Thank you, Rich, for your selfless and joyful service throughout numerous workshops, seminars, long conversations and for your valuable insights and suggestions for The Oracle. I greatly admire the integrity of your marriage and the trust that exists between you and your lovely wife, Linda, that has allowed you and I to be the best of friends.

Thank you, Madelene Toner, for your friendship and valuable help, love and support in countless ways. Your insights brought important changes to the story that were initially over looked during the critical developmental stages.

Thank you, Bram and Gaelyn Larrick of Lightbourne Images, and especially Gaelyn whose beautiful artistic talents gave birth to a wonderful book cover.

Thank you, Mary and David Dohrman of Lightworks!, whose sensitivity to the nature of The Oracle gave rise to a superb job of editing. Your expertise truly smoothed out the rough edges of the story.

Thank you, Penny Hancock of Griffin Publishing whose caring support and suggestions made the journey a lot easier.

Thank you, Linda Schooler, whose loving support became available when it was deeply needed. You have become a wonderful, faithful friend who has never placed great expectations on me.

Thank you, Robert Perala, a very special friend whose generosity and support of my work helped make the tough times less of a struggle.

And deep heart-felt thanks to Donna Henry, Ron Reig, Paulette Pitner, Dr. Richard Boylan, Ron Cusson, and Sophia Tiers. Your special support, acknowledgment, and encouragement truly carried me through some very rough times. May God and Goddess bless you all.

The Oracle of Clarion
is dedicated to my parents
Betty Jean and Richard Kenneth Mailhes
with all my love

ONE

S trange sounds jolted me from a dreamy sleep and I found myself in an unfamiliar bed. I squinted through heavy eyelids, but the surroundings remained fuzzy and puzzling. The peculiar beeping of some inhuman thing emanated from a blurry shape nearby. As I turned my head to get a look at whatever the thing was, a shocking, riveting pain tore through my neck. Grimacing with agony, I was hesitant to move again.

Where was I and how did I get here? As my vision cleared, dim patterns on the ceiling came into sharper focus. Light streamed in through a sliver of an opening in white curtains that hung all around me. I became aware of something wrapped about my neck and felt a hard obstacle in my throat. It would not budge after several swallows. Grumbling in silence, I carefully shifted my eyes and could now see the source of the annoying sounds. The strange beeping was coming from an electronic monitoring system used in hospital emergency rooms.

A hospital! My God, this is a hospital. Stunned, my mind buzzed and thoughts raced as I tried to remember. How did I get here? What happened? This is no place for an important dignitary. There are enormous responsibilities to attend to. The American people are counting on me! They must know that all is well and that the nation is secure. The people must not endure any uncertainty with the country's administration!

Where is my aide when I need him? Where is Murphy? Thoughts roared so loudly in my head that I was sure that someone would hear and come rushing in response. No one came and I found myself speechless for the first time in over thirty years of public service. I was unable to utter a word. As I lay in silence, my attention was drawn to some-one shuffling about on the other side of the curtains. *How long have they been there? Why haven't they checked on me? After all, I am a damn important person! I need to have answers! And what caused this hellish thing in my throat and this tightness in my neck?*

Get a grip on yourself, man . . . I reprimanded myself, as I recalled the medical examiner's recent diagnosis of high blood pressure. Coaching myself to relax, I closed my eyes and a vivid scene flashed before me.

There was an immense crowd, swelling with incessant loud and boisterous cheering while a contemporary live band blared a popular tune. I was being hurried along the sidewalk with Murphy and seven other guards surrounding me tightly as we approached the entrance to the convention center. The crowd had been unusually pressing, and rowdy onlookers were pushed behind boundary lines, enforced by a thick wall of city police.

One young man broke through and thrust his arm between guards, grasping at my suit. He was seized instantly by two policeman, and ushered away. Unruffled, and managing to maintain my dignified public image, I continued to smile and wave even though the intensity of the crowd was alarming.

Suddenly, there was confusion and screaming. Some-one burst through the envelopment of guards to my left, and before I could turn to face the disturbance, a deafening shot rang out. Searing pain ripped through my neck and shoulder. Then nothing, just nothing. And now here I was in the hospital. How long had it been? Finally, the realiza-

weariness consumed me. *Surgery and then what? How long would I need to be in the hospital? Taylor is a competent Vice President; however . . .*

Concern over the bureaucratic complexities of Taylor assuming the Presidency was overwhelming, and I drifted off into deep sleep for an unknown passage of time.

I returned to dim wakefulness when a queer, tingling sensation, similar to an electrical charge, permeated every fiber of my being. The feeling was weird, yet quite wonderful. The lids of my eyes felt weighted, and I could only open them enough to glimpse what appeared to be an illuminated figure standing next to me. It was a woman, gently laying her warm and strangely vibrating hands on my body.

Turning my head slightly, I squinted with effort and could vaguely make out tall pine trees a short distance away. The fragrance of wild flowers was delightful, and the soothing rays of a bright yellow sun felt invigorating. The sky was a deep vibrant blue, the way it often appears at high altitude, while soft, fluffy clouds floated lazily over the treetops. The air was cool and crisp as if washed clean by a recent spring storm.

I was feeling marvelous and thought of rising to greet this person standing next to me. When my eyes fully opened, I was startled to find myself staring into the luminous face of a extraordinarily beautiful woman. Then my body jerked, and in a flash I found myself right back in the hospital bed!

A dream — it was only a dream. But what an amazing dream! It was so vivid, so real that my body was still quaking with the energy that vibrated through the woman's hands. How incredible to have a dream like that. I don't think I've ever had one quite like it before.

My contemplation was broken when I noticed a thick silence enveloping me. I looked through the opening in the curtains, straining for any indication that the others were nearby. All I could see was that the door of my room was wide open, and the lights in the hall seemed unusually bright. High partitions surrounding the nurse's station obscured my view, and made it difficult to see anyone.

My throat no longer felt dry, and when I turned my head, my neck and shoulder were free of pain. I was deeply grateful. As I returned my gaze to the open door, a small boy entered the room as if he knew exactly where he was going and marched right up to the side of the bed.

"I was told that the President of the United States was here and I've been sent to greet you in person," he announced boldly, as if he was a representative of a very important council.

Bewildered, I gawked at him. His face was sweet and innocent like that of a little angel. His large, pale blue eyes were fathomless with a wisdom far beyond his age, which I guessed to be about seven. With glowing skin and a tousle of blonde hair, he was the healthiest looking kid I had ever seen.

Murphy had assured me that the entire floor had been vacated of patients for security reasons, and so I asked, "How did you get in here, young man?"

"I just walked in. Nobody stopped me or asked any questions, so I figured it was all right. Besides, I heard you say one time on television that you loved children, and so I thought it would be okay to come and see you since I'm a child." He replied with cheery anticipation, searching my face for acceptance, and quietly waited for my response.

I recalled those times when I was encouraged by supporters to make specific statements to the public to increase my popularity, and ensure my nomination for the presidency. I liked kids. After all, I had raised my own. Being in my sixties and fully devoted to public service, however, had necessitated a life style that did not include small children, except for occasional family gatherings. Even then, my attention was largely taken up by adults. In many ways, I had forgotten what it was like to relate to children, and how much I had lost touch with my childlike playfulness years ago when my own children left home. Over time, I found myself becoming increasingly impatient and intolerant of children's crying, whining, fidgeting, and other unadult-like behavior.

"Well," I sighed in resignation, "I suppose it's all right for you to visit for a moment. Where are your mother and father? You know, they may be worried about you right now. You should go find them. It was nice to meet you, and I appreciate that you came all this way to say hello. But, I think you've been gone long enough from your parents." I caught my breath, and only then realized I had been talking. My voice was back! Surgery must have taken place, and the injury successfully repaired. And there was no pain, no discomfort anywhere in my body.

"This is fantastic!" Blurting out in excitement, I called loudly, "Murphy! Where's Murphy? He's got to know." I glanced at the little boy. "He'll be so pleased. My Presidency will prevail after all. With a few short days of careful rest in the hospital, I'll be up and around in no time. Murphy!"

"I'm really glad you're feeling better . . . " Calmly responding, this small fellow persisted in gaining my attention. His eyes looked down at the floor for a moment as if sad about something. " . . . and don't worry, I don't think my parents are worrying about me. I take care of myself pretty well. And besides, I came here to show you something." He looked up again, his pale blue eyes brightening with excitement.

"Before you show me that something, tell me your name, young man." I groped for some simple conversation.

"Mathias. It's pronounced with a long 'i' as in 'eye'."

He pointed to his eye in a serious manner that caused me to chuckle.

"Well now, Mathias with a long 'i', what have you to show me?" Managing a fleeting grin, I warned, "You had best make it quick, for someone will come soon to take you back to your parents."

He ran to the opposite side of the bed, slipped his small hand into mine, and pulled hard, urging me to get up. An innocent kid's game, I thought. He doesn't realize that I need quiet and rest.

"Son, I can't get out of bed just yet." As he tugged on my arm, my mind raced ahead to the day I would be released from the hospital.

"Divine Mother says you can get up *now*." He stuck out his jaw in determination, and yanked even harder. "Get up! You'll see."

"Who is Divine Mother? Sounds like a religious deity to me. If she's a friend of yours, she obviously doesn't know what has happened to me." I stared at the ceiling, trying to ignore his persistence.

While he continued to pull on me, I focused my attention on my body and became aware of an unusual feeling of lightness. And so I slowly sat up, careful not to strain anything. Was I being foolish in letting Mathias sway me into getting up too soon? I cautiously felt my neck and shoulders. The bandages were in place, but there was no pain. I looked about me and noticed that the whole room seemed brighter in an odd sort of way.

"Divine Mother says your injury is healed, and you can take off the bandages," he announced confidently.

After eyeing him suspiciously, I complied. I quickly unraveled the bandages, lest I get caught by Murphy or one of the patrolling nurses, and dumped it all in a heap on the bed. Slowly reaching up to explore the damaged area, I discovered a mere lump on the side of my neck.

No wound, no stitches. I was dumbfounded.

"What goes on here young man? Who is Divine Mother? And come to think of it, why hasn't anyone come in here to check on me? Where's Murphy?" I called out sharply, "Murphy! Come here at once!" No one responded.

Furious, I bellowed, "Security, indeed! Is this any way to protect the President of the United States? American taxpayers are footing the bill for my hospitalization and security measures! They better well know that I've got proper care and protection! Anyone could come in here and get away with murder. This is an outrage. Murphy!" My face flushed with angry heat.

"No one can hear you, and Divine Mother says you better calm down before your blood pressure goes up." Mathias folded his arms across his chest, like a father who was greatly frustrated with his unruly child. Who was this little boy? He didn't seem to be normal. He actually glowed with a faint light that emanated from him.

I let down the railing from my bed and swung my legs over. Feeling no discomfort, I dangled my legs, and looked at the floor with apprehension. If I step down, will I be able to stand safely? Might as well give it a try. "Come closer, Mathias, and let me steady myself on your shoulder."

With his help I stood up without wavering. Embarrassed to discover that the hospital gown didn't cover my bare behind, I bunched the open back together with one hand and set about to find more suitable covering.

"There has to be a robe around here somewhere— perhaps in that closet. Murphy! I need you right now! Nurse! Doctor! Security!" The lack of response was exasperating, and when no one heeded my shouting, I opened the closet and found clothes that belonged to someone else.

"Put them on, they'll fit you perfectly," Mathias urged with certainty. "You'll need these clothes for your disguise. Better hurry! Divine Mother is waiting."

"Young man, are you telling the President what to do? Who is this Divine Mother, and what has she got to do with all of this?" I was becoming quite annoyed with the boldness of this little boy. How would the headline look on the front page of the New York Global Times: "President of The United States Defers Sound Judgement to Small, Mysterious Child"?

I dressed quickly in the adjoining bathroom, and was surprised to find that the clothes fit so well. Stepping out, I posed briefly for Mathias, and he applauded the outfit: a coarsely woven wool sweater pulled over a soft turtleneck shirt, faded blue jeans, and well-worn but comfortable running shoes. I searched the room, and rummaged recklessly through the cabinet drawers for my wallet and glasses.

"Divine Mother says you won't need your glasses or any of that other stuff," Mathias said in a confident manner.

"What do you mean ? I've worn glasses for years. I need them. And I need my wallet because it has all the documents that identify who I am." Muttering, I kept on rummaging. " 'Won't need any of that other stuff ' — indeed!"

With great surprise, he asked, "You don't know who you are without documents?" And as he said this, Mathias cocked his head quizzically to one side as if he were listening to someone.

"Divine Mother says that your real identity doesn't have anything to do with documents or how others think of you. So you'll have to leave behind your old identity because you can't take it with you. After Divine Mother is through with you, your new identity will help you to make important transformations in yourself and in the world. You won't need your glasses either, because you'll need to throw away your old way of looking at things so you can see yourself and the world condition in a new way."

"What are you talking about? You're not making any sense at all. And it's time for you to tell me who this Divine Mother is," I demanded defiantly, feeling a bit silly for becoming so defensive with a child.

"She can tell you about that better than I can. Divine Mother has an extremely important message for all the people of the world. She says she really needs to talk with you because the world and all the people in it are in big trouble! And because you're a very important per-son, you can make awesome changes happen. She's very powerful but she needs your help. She came into the room just before I did, and I know you felt her power." He let out a long sigh, as though convincing me was a much bigger job than he thought it would be.

"I don't remember anyone coming into this room before you arrived. It's necessary that you tell me the truth, young man." Scolding him gently, I shook my finger for emphasis.

"Don't you feel better? You were hurt real bad before Divine Mother healed you. She came as a great light and put all the nurses and guards to sleep so that she could do her miracle. You've been healed!" Mathias yanked on my hand, "Look at yourself! Look in the mirror!"

Skeptically, I stepped over to a full length mirror on the wall, looked at myself, and gasped. I appeared to be at least fifteen years younger! All the trials and pressures of the Presidency were gone from my face! There were fewer gray hairs; and those which remained were bright, shimmering threads of silver-white.

"What goes on here? I *do* feel different." I remembered the strange dream I had of the beautiful woman and the incredible tingling sensation. Looking at Mathias intently, I said, "I think I'd like to meet this Divine Mother."

"Wow! Then let's go." Hopping up and down, he ran

to the open door with gleeful excitement. "We haven't got much time. They're still asleep out here. We need to leave now."

I followed him out into the larger room and nurse's station, and found Murphy, my personal guards, the doctor and hospital staff sound asleep: some lay sprawled in their chairs, while others slumped over their desks. How could this be? It was absurd and impossible. Was I having an altered state experience, or had I been given some drug that induces hallucinations? I bent over and looked Murphy in the face while he blithely snored away, and reached out to touch him.

"Stop! You'll wake him up if you do that." Whispering excitedly, Mathias kept flapping his hands wildly in the air. "We've got to go!"

Keeping my voice to an agitated whisper, I rasped, "It would be foolish of me to go anywhere with you, young man. I cannot leave these people, and jeopardize my safety. I have a whole country to consider." Befuddled, I mumbled, "Why am I whispering?"

"But Divine Mother is waiting . . . " His lower lip protruded in a pout and his little shoulders slumped in a sad way that touched me. Grasping his arms gently, I looked squarely into his eyes.

"Mathias," speaking slowly, I searched for the kindest words possible. "I don't know who this Divine Mother is. Obviously there is something unusual going on, and there seems to be something quite special about her. However, I have tremendous responsibilities, and I cannot go running about with a small boy on some wild adventure. The American people will think I've gone daft and become unfit for the Presidency. As charming as you are, young man, I will have to decline."

"Well . . . then . . . I guess I'll have to show you this."

He reached into his jacket, and struggled to free something from the pocket. "Divine Mother says this ought to convince you."

He placed the object in my hand, and my mouth fell open. "How can this be? Where did you get this?"

Mathias said nothing as I stared in astonishment at the object in my palm. "Why, this is the gold lapel pin my mother had designed especially for me while she was in Europe. But, I never wore it because I was uncomfortable with its religious meaning. The Baptist Church had been the religious foundation for my adult years. My mother had been raised a Catholic, but she had begun to dabble in the Ancient Theosophies and New Age teachings. She had this lapel pin specifically made in the image of Mother Mary."

The figure was finely crafted in flowing folds of gold with arms slightly outstretched, palms facing outward, and bare feet resting upon a crescent moon nestled among clusters of stars. The face portrayed true peace and serenity.

"She told me . . . " I stopped, on the verge of tears as I recalled the voice of my mother, " . . . that Mother Mary was vastly different than the Virgin Mary depicted in the Bible. She said that Mother Mary, in truth, was the earthly and physical embodiment of the Divine Mother Goddess. My dear mother assured me that Mother Mary's eternal compassion and love would always protect me. Even though the pin was exquisite in design and beautifully crafted, I just couldn't bring myself to wear it, and kept it instead in a carved wooden box. My mother was quite hurt that I did this. Later, a fire burned our entire house to the ground and the pin was never found. When my mother died I had regrets that I never wore the pin, just to make her happy, and an even deeper regret about losing it. There is no lapel pin like this on the face of the earth. How did you come by it?"

Mathias remained silent as I turned the pin over. Yes, there was no doubt about it— the inscription was there. I wistfully read out loud, "Blessed, loved, and protected art thou, Clarion, all the days of your life."

"Who's Clarion?" Mathias queried.

"That's my first name," I told him. It was something I rarely heard at all since becoming President. I was usually addressed as President Agate, my dear President, Mr. President, or sir. I rather missed being called by the name my mother had given me.

"Isn't that a girl's name?" Mathias wrinkled his nose as he questioned.

Amused, I replied, "Not really. My mother claimed that she could hear the heavenly trumpets of angels when I was born, and when she looked upon my tiny face she heard the words, 'A brilliantly clear spirit that will heed the clarion call to action'."

I would always giggle with embarrassment whenever my mother told that story during my childhood. Now I recalled the story with great fondness.

"I like it. Can I call you Clarion?" he asked shyly, with eyes that twinkled like that of a mischievous elf.

Gazing warmly at him with tears of old memories swelling in my eyes, I said, "Why not? I feel younger and a lot less serious when people call me by my first name." As Mathias grinned broadly, I saw in his face a flash of something oddly familiar, and for a moment, I was lost in his eyes.

"Let's hurry. We can be back before anyone knows you're gone." He grabbed my arm and pulled hard, but all I could do was stand motionless while staring at the lapel pin in my hand.

"Don't you want to help the people of the world to become happier? Don't you want to heal the planet? Please,

Clarion!" Mathias pleaded, "Divine Mother will teach you many powerful things that will help you help everyone! Do it for all us kids of the world so we can grow up in a safe place of love and peace."

I shifted my gaze to that glowing little face, and felt my heart pounding, as if something exciting and wonderful was about to happen. My feet began moving as if they had a mind of their own while Mathias, holding onto my hand tightly, led me through double doors that opened into a long, wide hallway.

Dazed and disoriented, I followed him past more sleeping guards and policemen. Down the corridor we went, and on to what was to become a daring and extraordinary venture into the unknown.

TWO

I don't know why I went with him. All logic and reason escaped me. Compelled by an unknown but powerful force, I felt a great sense of urgency. Could this Divine Mother shed crucial insight on present world dilemmas? Is her wisdom reliable enough to assist me in my mission to help humanity?

Perhaps I'm insane, or maybe all of this is just a dream. But as we made our way to the elevator and rode it down to the main lobby, I let the responsibilities of the Presidency fade into the background. My curiosity about this mystery woman and what she could offer seemed to bear greater importance.

When the doors opened to the noise and hustle of a busy hospital lobby, I panicked and rammed my fist hard on the elevator function button. The doors snapped shut and I fell back against the wall, gasping for breath.

"Those people out there are not asleep," I croaked between gasps. "I can't be sure that it's safe for me to go walking about without security after what I've been through. That would-be assassin may have accomplices who will make sure that the job is finished!"

"You have your Mother Mary pin, don't you?" Mathias jerked on my sleeve. "You'll be protected. It's true! You're an important person. Nothing bad will happen to you. Put the lapel pin on, and put on those sunglasses that are in your pants pocket."

There were no sunglasses in the pocket before. Yet when I put my hand in the pocket, there they were.

"Ridiculous! None of this is making any sense." Grumbling, I fumbled with the sunglasses, nervously adjusted them on my face, and attached the pin to the sweater. I felt rather childish, as though I was playing some kind of crazy charade. Taking a few deep breaths, I collected myself, and pressed the "open door" button.

We bolted out of the elevator and scurried along the corridor toward a glass-paned exit which opened onto the street. As we approached coat racks on the wall, a well-worn, Australian bush hat caught my eye. Grabbing it as we passed by, I dropped it onto my head, tucked a few hairs underneath, and hoped that no one would come running after this thief. No one pursued, and we found ourselves standing on a busy sidewalk looking up and down the crowded street.

"Now what?" Incredulous, I found myself awaiting instructions from a kid.

Mathias tossed his head back in a wild guffaw. "You look like Indiana Jones!"

My lips curled in disapproval, which only brought more laughter.

Still snickering, he commanded, "Quick. Get in this car!" He opened the door of an old brown sedan that still operated on gasoline. A curious looking man was at the wheel. Puffing laboriously on a fat cigar, he seemed expectant of our arrival and gestured for us to get into the back seat. I stood and stared at him, wondering if he could be trusted.

"Clarion! Get in! It's okay. He's a friend of mine." Mathias jumped into the back seat, slid across to the other side, and begged me to follow.

Here I was, about to do something very foolish.

Would anyone with only a smattering of intelligence have gone this far? My eyes were riveted on the driver until a flash of movement caught my eye. I looked up the street in the direction of the motion and saw three men in dark suits running toward me. Leaping into the back seat, I slammed the door shut as the driver sped away, tires screeching. We filed into busy traffic on the boulevard. Looking back through the rear window, I saw the men stop dead where the car had left the curb while they watched us until we were out of sight. Who were they? Did I just escape another assassination attempt?

Slumping into the seat, I let out a sigh of relief and remarked, "I can't believe this is happening." I looked at Mathias, and was surprised to see a big smile on his face, as though he had accomplished his mission and was having a great time.

"Sir," I called up to the driver. "Would you mind telling me what this is all about? I'm greatly confused. I believe that you may have the advantage. Can you help me out?"

The driver did not answer, but continued to concentrate on the road ahead. When I opened my mouth to speak again, Mathias stopped me.

"He can't hear and can't talk. Its okay, though. He's a special man who's married to a nice lady and has lots of adopted orphans at home. He'll take good care of us. Really!" Mathias said, trying to comfort me.

Well, I thought, at least it might be easier for me to travel incognito in this car. No one would go looking for a VIP in such a battered old automobile. I had grown accustomed to the luxury of the modern hydro-powered air borne vehicles, and was spoiled with their smooth, quiet ride. However, not everyone could afford the new vehicles. Even though the early years of the 21st century were filled with astounding technological advances, the old gas-powered autos were slow to be replaced.

We sat in silence, rolling along at a speedy clip, while the scape of the city dwindled into suburbs and large, vacant lots. Most of the time I gazed out the window, not daring to think about the trouble I was getting into. Turning often to study the road behind us for suspicious vehicles, I was satisfied that we were safe for the time being. It became easier for me to relax.

Mathias seemed content to watch the passing scenery, and the driver quietly puffed away on his third cigar. Glad that the windows were partially rolled down, I watched as the thick, grey smoke curled upward to vanish to the outside.

The highway traffic gradually thinned out as we passed farmland and approached the foothills. I suddenly realized what a beautiful day it was. Unusually clear, sharp colors pervaded the landscape, creating an almost surreal image. Everything looked rich and vibrant. I felt younger and more vital, and contemplated the strange events of the day. If this was a dream I expected to be waking up soon.

"It's not a dream. This is real," Mathias quipped confidently. "You're simply being more of your true, natural self. That's why you look younger, and why you feel so good, and why all the colors are brighter. Deep down inside, you're enjoying all of this. You've always wanted to have some genuine adventure in your life. You've always wanted something truly exciting to happen. That's why you used to read so many mystery novels and adventure stories."

"How did you know what I was thinking? And how did you know I like to read mystery novels and adventure stories?" I hadn't had time to read such books since my public service responsibilities had taken a quantum leap. Fiction had a wonderful way of taking my mind off my

work, and I missed being able to engross myself thorough-
ly in it. Marveling at this little boy who seemed to be a step
ahead of me, I wondered if he was a midget secret agent in
disguise, only masquerading as a young child.

"I knew what you were thinking in the same way I
knew about the Mother Mary pin that your mother gave
you. Divine Mother speaks to me and tells me things." He
went on to look out the window, apparently undisturbed by
my concern.

"Now tell me, Mathias, who is this Divine Mother?
After coercing me to go with you by way of some rather
convincing demonstrations, don't you think its about time
I had a little more information?"

"Well," he responded thoughtfully. "I don't know
where to start. All I know is that Divine Mother is like God
in a lot of ways. Some people say that she is the feminine
part of God, and that she's coming back to the world to
bring healing to the hearts of all the people. She has a lot
of love and compassion. She's also very powerful. When
she speaks to me I hear her inside. I feel warm, and I know
she really cares about me. She makes my heart smile real
big!" Mathias drew an imaginary smile across his chest
with his finger and looked up at me.

Returning the smile, I found myself becoming quite
captivated with this little man. His eyes were large, round
and full of that strange and wonderful familiarity I had
noticed before. "So, how do you hear Divine Mother in-
side of you?"

"I just go within and turn my attention to the inside
of me. I become very still, and then I listen. Even when
I'm busy doing things, I can hear her because I've practiced
at becoming calm inside. Anyone can hear her. Most people
simply don't take the time. They're all too busy with things
that take their attention away from that inside place, in the
heart, where the soul is.

"The soul always knows how to hear Divine Mother and how to hear God. The soul is like a part of God that lives in the heart and is very personal. The soul remembers God. Most people don't make the soul very important, and they forget about it. They live without deep meaning in their lives and wonder why they don't feel very much joy. They don't understand why they aren't fulfilled and happy. Lots of people die of old age wondering why their lives weren't more rewarding, and they have a lot of regret. Its kind of sad that people don't choose to let their soul guide them. This would be a much happier world if we all did that." Mathias stared out the window the entire time he spoke, as if in a trance.

I watched his small face, curious as to how such wisdom could be spoken by a young child. As I thought about his words, I remembered my long involvement with the Baptist Church and the years of searching through a variety of religions. My perspectives changed greatly over the years — the teachings of organized religions had lost their meaning for me. Nevertheless, I longed for a connection with the powerful goodness that appeared to be present in *all* religions.

God had always been an enigma to me. But somehow I felt closer to God in the churches and temples no matter how much I disagreed with their teachings. I hungered for a more meaningful and tangible representation of God, something that I could apply to myself, my life, my work, and to the world. I could not find God in the real world. There was endless strife, struggle and despair. There was so much unhappiness, war, starvation, poverty, greed . . . and politics. Where was God in all of this?

Bumps in the road jolted me out of my musings, and I became aware that we were still in the car, traveling along a highway which had turned into a narrow, winding country road. We were into the foothills and climbing higher.

Surprised to feel content in this moment, I felt as though I belonged with this little boy, trekking into some unknown reality. I had given hardly any thought about Murphy and all the people back at the hospital. Were they still sleeping, or had they awakened to find that their President had disappeared? Imagining the scene, my hand stifled the escape of a gleeful chuckle. Of course, the dis-appearance of a President could jeopardize national security. Murphy will go mad with worry. My daughter will be devastated. The American people will be uncertain about the strength and safety of their country. I began to feel enormously guilty.

"Guilt will only make you grow older faster," Mathias scolded. "If you keep thinking like that, you'll lose your good feelings and aliveness. The colors won't seem as bright and beautiful. The world will look dull and boring; and you won't be able to hear God, Divine Mother, or even your own soul!" Indeed, as I glanced out the window I noticed that the radiance of the day did seem to have paled.

"Young man, it can be most uncomfortable to have someone reading one's thoughts! How can anyone have any privacy?" I protested loudly. I didn't want to admit that he may be right. Certainly the day appears different than before, when I noticed the vibrancy of colors. I no longer felt as good as I did before. In fact, I felt tired.

"People feel guilty because they think they've been bad and they've done something wrong." Mathias continued, "Divine Mother says that when people feel guilty, they lose their connection with God. And the more guilt they feel, the more unhappy they are. People will never have peace of mind as long as they carry guilt around with them."

"People *should* feel guilty if they've committed a violation, Mathias," I decreed smugly. "That's simply a common-sense moral value."

"Divine Mother says that guilt is created by people, not by God. She says that when people separated from God a long time ago, guilt was created, and people stopped respecting and trusting each other. In order to control those who were hurting others and behaving in destructive ways, laws were made to punish them and to make them feel guilty. The idea was to make people feel bad enough about what they did so that they would stop doing bad things.

"Some people want to control others by making them feel guilty. Divine Mother says that when people come back to God, respect and trust will return and no one will hurt anyone anymore. They'll stop hurting the animals and stop hurting the earth, too. When there are trust and respect, there is no need for guilt!" As Mathias spoke, his eyes reflected not only his great intensity, but also a deep wisdom that belied his age.

Leaning back, I marveled at how the conversation had meandered into such a deep subject. Considering the words that were given to Mathias by Divine Mother, I thought about the methods of punishment used as a means of controlling those who violated others. It had long been realized that the penal system in America was inadequate and did little or nothing to eliminate crime.

Lobbyists had pushed for years to reform this penal system, and the beaucracy fought them every step of the way. I had experienced heavy pressures from both sides. No wonder it has taken so long to change things in this country. Too many have been afraid of change even though the present system was no longer working. Too many have continued to believe that the way we've always done things, through the established institutional systems, would provide security. I remembered the reform proposals that I had yet to review, stacked high on the secretary's desk, and knew that the penal system reforms were among them.

These thoughts vanished when the car bounced roughly over some dips in the road. I noticed that we had turned off the highway and were proceeding on a dirt road that climbed higher into the mountains.

"Mathias," I spoke softly, "if Divine Mother supposedly came to the hospital and performed some miracle on me, why do we have to drive so far to see her? Why couldn't she just talk to me in the hospital? Why all this suspense?"

He watched the passing trees through the window. "Well," he began, "if people have never learned to quiet and calm their minds, or to really listen, it's much harder for them to go inside and hear Divine Mother or God, especially when they live in a crowded city. Divine Mother says that there are dark and heavy energy fields in cities, caused by huge amounts of fear, doubt and stress. If someone living in the city tries to hear Divine Mother while they still have a lot of fear and doubt, its like trying to listen to a radio station that has noisy static. All that static makes it harder to hear the words and the music. Divine Mother and God speak to everyone all the time, but no one hears them because of all the static — from all the fear, stress and doubt. We're going high up into the mountains where it will be much easier for you to hear her. She has many important things to say to you. She believes that you can help change the world in a big way."

"Then I assume she lives in the mountains and — "

"Oh, no! Divine Mother lives everywhere," Mathias broke in. "We're going up into the mountains because there is a special place where you can meet her. It's a secret and sacred place where she will appear to you in a real physical body! You'll like it there. It's beautiful and peaceful."

As we climbed higher, wisps of puffy white clouds raced overhead, indicating a strong breeze at the higher

26

elevations. The driver, who had not looked once at us during our journey, navigated the winding mountain road as if he had driven it a thousand times.

The old sedan groaned and strained, the engine laboring with the increasing altitude, and I grew concerned that we might not make it to our destination, wherever that was.

As I thought about the Divine Mother, I wondered why I was treating this whole event as if she were a queen, commanding my presence to her royal court like an obedient servant. Could all of this simply be an illusion?

My hand went up to touch the Mother Mary pin. It was certainly no illusion! It was one of a kind, and there was no other like it. How had this come to be? My curiosity about Divine Mother stirred an adventuresome spirit within me. This was no ordinary day, nor was this an ordinary little boy seated beside me. My guilt faded as I looked forward to meeting Divine Mother, and to having some important questions answered.

We turned onto another road — a thin strip of beige that sliced its way through a dim, thick forest. Branches stretched across the edge of the road, barely allowing enough room on either side for the old car to pass. As we continued on, the trees increased their encroachment upon the road, scraping the sides of the car while blocking out a good portion of the daylight. Small patches of bright green meadows, alive and vibrant with wild flowers, flashed brilliantly through the tangled mesh as we drove on.

Rolling down the window, I caught the fresh scents of pine and cedar. Cool, moist air blew in through the window. It felt refreshing on my face, and I took several more deep breaths before looking at Mathias, who had been looking at me.

"You look happy, Clarion. Aren't you glad you came with me?" He beamed with an innocence that warmed my heart.

"I *am* enjoying the scenery and it *is* beautiful here. But, I'm still not sure why I've allowed this to happen. The shock from the assassination attempt must have affected my judgment, since I seem to have lost all common sense. If this Divine Mother really came to visit me in the hospital and is responsible for my miraculous recovery, did she also do something to interfere with my good judgment?" Even as I spoke, I found these words hard to believe. For some reason I knew that this Divine Mother had good intentions, and that she may have some remarkable abilities. Mathias said nothing, and returned his gaze to the forest outside.

A quiet moment passed before he softly spoke, "When you let your heart guide you, things stop making sense to your mind. Divine Mother says you can't intellectualize a feeling and you can't intellectualize love. She says that people get into their heads far too often, and they analyze so many things that really belong to the realm of the heart. She says that people stop being open to the joy and wonder of life when they become serious, hard working adults. Most grown-ups believe that wonderment and joy are only for children. They don't follow their hearts, and they lack enthusiasm. Most people experience very little joy and play throughout their entire lives!

"Divine Mother says too many people spend their creative energy working at jobs they don't like all that much, just to earn money so they can buy things, collect possessions, and keep up with the Joneses. Then they die all tired and unfulfilled in their hearts, wondering why they never let themselves realize their hopes and dreams. And mostly, all they have to show for their hard work is a lot of stuff they have to leave behind." Mathias shook his head with empathy.

"You're just following your heart, Clarion, that's all!" He brightened as he added, "Your heart, where the soul lives, is guiding you. Your soul knows that this adventure is really for your highest good; and as long as you let your soul guide you, you will find what's needed to help you become the person you were really meant to be. To be true to yourself means to follow your heart and soul. This will bring joy and inspiration to you. Hasn't Divine Mother inspired you already with her miracles? Don't you feel drawn to her like a magnet? You could have said 'No' to me back there in the hospital and stayed. But you would never have known about Divine Mother, and you would have missed out on a great adventure!"

I had to admit that it was quite startling, even annoying, to hear this young boy speak with such extraordinary insight. It seemed as though I was the child and he was the wise old sage! Folding my arms across my chest in a manner befitting a snob, I refused to respond to him.

After a long period of silence, the car approached an entrance of some sort. Iron gates which hung on huge flagstone pillars were standing open to either side, and we passed through them to whatever awaited us beyond.

"Are we here?" I blurted out. "Is this where I finally get to meet this mysterious person?"

"We're almost there. You'll get to see the sanctuary, too, and the gardens and streams. There's a big pond with orange and gold fish. I love it here! It's my second home." Mathias spoke with great anticipation, as if we were arriving at an amusement park.

"You called this your second home . . . where is your real home?" I queried, surprised that I had not asked him this before.

"I'll tell you soon. There's so much for you to learn, and so much Divine Mother has to tell you. It's really important that you listen to what she has to say. The survival of the world and all the people depends on who will listen and heed her messages. The future happiness of the children depends on the choices made by the grown-ups. You've got to help them make better choices or else everything in the world will get very dark and very sad." Mathias looked down, his chin close to his chest. His angelic radiance seemed to fade and flicker as he voiced his deep concern for the world.

"There, there, Mathias. Things aren't all that bad in the world, are they?" Patting him lightly on the head, I didn't believe a word I said, yet felt it was my responsibility to reassure this innocent, vulnerable child.

The driver slowed the sedan as we rounded a circular driveway and arrived at another entrance. This time the gates were closed. We stepped out of the car and stood before a pair of heavy wooden gates supported by high, white stone walls. The driver immediately pulled away, and I turned quickly to wave, regretting that I was unable to thank him.

Thank him for what? Who knows what I may be getting myself into by letting him drive me to who-knows-where?

"Is he returning later to take us home?" I bent over to look Mathias in the eyes. "When is he returning, and how long are we going to stay here? I really must be getting back to the hospital before dark. I have a job to do, an entire country to run. I have incredible obligations! I have to— "

Mathias held a finger to his lips and shushed my rising voice. I stood there bewildered, unable to figure out why he had this effect on me, as though I were in kindergarten again.

"This is a sacred place. Shouting or sharp words aren't allowed. This is a special place of peace and healing. There's a holy presence on these grounds. You can really feel it if you're calm and respectful. We'll have to ring the bell, though, so Lola knows we're here." Mathias stretched his arm, teetering on the tips of his toes, to reach the small wooden toggle on the end of a thin rope.

     Lola? What kind of a name is that for someone who lives in a "sacred" place? This could be interesting, I mused.

THREE

The bell rang out with low gong-like reverberations that sent shivers up my spine. Footsteps were heard on the other side of the wall, and the large bolts on the gated entrance slid open with a loud scraping sound. Whoever the greeter might be, I decided that it would be wise to keep my identity a secret, just to play it safe.

"Mathias," I whispered, "Don't say anything about who I am, do you understand? I'll answer any questions put to me in that regard. Agreed?"

"Yeah, but — " Mathias stopped short when one side of the gate swung inward. A slender, attractive, fiftyish-looking woman appeared, displaying a sweet, welcoming smile and sparkling eyes.

"I am so pleased that you came! I'm Lola." She held out her hand and I took it gingerly, introducing myself only as Clarion. A child-like giggle popped from her mouth as she added, "Please, come this way and I will take you inside."

She gestured for us to follow while she weaved her way through a glorious rose garden, precisely stepping on the broad, flat stones that paved our way. The smell of roses was thick and intoxicating, and an uncontrollable grin crept across my face until I was sure that my mouth stretched far beyond its normal boundaries!

I watched Lola as she walked, her hips swaying easily for a woman of her age. Her obvious relaxation made me aware of the stiffness of my own stride. While the two of them walked ahead of me, I tried to imitate the easy swing of her hips, hoping no one would look back to catch me in the act of being undignified.

The colors were vibrant and bright. I recalled what Mathias had said about my attitude and how it could change my perception of the world. What was causing me to feel so giddy? Whatever it was, I was enjoying it.

We passed through a smaller gate, flanked on either side by tall, dense hedges. Hiking up a grass covered knoll, we approached a huge and unusual looking rustic house of wood, secluded among a grove of redwoods. As we came close, the shift in atmosphere around the house called forth a feeling of sanctuary.

The architecture portrayed a slight oriental theme, with colossal beams of blonde wood serving as the main buttress points in strategic areas. We climbed up a few steps to the wooden deck, which appeared to surround the entire house, and I marveled at the intricate carvings on the overhead beams and on the large, vertical supports. On closer inspection, the engravings revealed a remarkable collage of fabulous flowers, animals of every kind, insects, birds, and water creatures, all blending into one continuous, flowing and harmonious pattern. Every wooden beam was different. I was mesmerized by the incredible detail of this art when Mathias spoke.

"We're ready to go in. Later we can look at the gardens. Right now, Lola wants to serve tea and something to eat. She makes her own teas and serves food only from the gardens. She's a pulmonary artist, you know!" Mathias announced, round-eyed and grinning.

"Mathias, that's *culinary* artist," Lola squealed in delight in response to Mathias' amusing misuse of the word. Giving him a quick hug, she turned to take my hand. "Come. Come in and relax. The atmosphere of this sacred place will soothe even the most worried of souls."

I followed them through a wide veranda and into a large and spacious living area with high vaulted ceilings. There was no furniture— only cushions stacked neatly in the corners, and a few low, teakwood tables that displayed an arrangement of fine china vases, fascinating statuary, and glorious fresh flowers.

The outer walls were made of movable partitions which were opened wide to reveal the luxurious gardens that enveloped this special place. Noticing Lola's silent request as she pointed first to our feet and then to the floor, we removed our shoes. The weave of the grass mat covering the floor felt good beneath my feet.

The ambience was one of simplicity, grace, restfulness and peace. Lola guided us into another spacious room where there was only one very large, low table with plush cushions set around it. We sat down as Lola quickly disappeared through a doorway behind the nearest wall. I gazed out into the garden and inhaled the fresh, cool air. I looked at Mathias and smiled with a nod of approval.

Mathias grinned and kept his hands folded on the table. Such a delightful little boy. His parents must be worried about him. Perhaps Lola is his guardian or relative. Maybe I need not be concerned about it.

As I looked out into the garden and studied the wide variety of flowers and shrubs, once again I was in awe of the vibrant colors. My attention was drawn to my own hands as I noticed the emanation of a faint golden glow. Then it vanished. Mathias giggled as I held up my hands, turning them this way and that in an attempt to recapture the sight.

"You really did see what you thought you saw." Still giggling, he added, "More life-force energy is moving through you; that's what you're seeing. You're getting a healing from all of this and becoming more natural.

You're enjoying this place so much that you're really opening up!"

I studied Mathias intently and was reminded of that same glow I saw around him when we first met in the hospital. The hospital and all of the events of the morning seemed far away and long ago. There was not one clock anywhere, and I guessed by the light of the day that it must be early afternoon, although it really should be much later than that. We must have traveled in the car for hours.

Why was I not more concerned about the responsibilities of the Presidency? That amusing, gleeful feeling emerged once more. I felt like a kid again, able to get away with something and hoping no one would find out.

Guilt was about to arise, when Lola quietly appeared with a lavish array of delicacies atop a huge tray. She set teapot, cups and servings of food upon the table with a graceful flair. The smell was enticing, and I realized I was famished. I hadn't thought of food all morning, and certainly I hadn't had any solid food while in the hospital. Most likely, the excitement of the day's events had quelled my need for something to eat.

I was eagerly waiting for our host to begin serving when she quietly suggested, "Let's join in a brief prayer and give thanks for the earth's bounty." Lola took Mathias' hand and reached for mine. As I clasped both their hands, I felt a bit sheepish. Here I was, facing this issue of prayer again and feeling rather hypocritical as I bowed my head.

I decided to be a gracious guest and be attentive as she spoke. While the words poured eloquently from Lola's mouth, a shiver went up my spine and an odd sensation of tingling warmth radiated from our clasped hands. Curious, I peeked through squinted eyes and saw the faint golden glow on Mathias and also on Lola. My own hands were again surrounded by this strange emanation. The tingling

sensation increased, and I was about to jerk my hands a-
way when Lola ended the prayer. She raised her eyes
slowly and looked directly into mine. Her knowing gaze
penetrated deeply, and I blushed.

Escaping her gaze, I looked appreciatively at the
food. "This setting is wonderful. Your preparation and ar-
rangement of everything is quite appetizing and appeal-
ing. I must say that I am anxious to taste all that I see here.
When may we begin?"

Lola beamed with modest pride as she served the tea,
then with a motion of her hand silently coaxed us to take our
own portions. We helped ourselves to a variety of colorful
marinated vegetables, succulent fresh fruits, exotic con-
diments, sweet breads and dates, all prepared in a simple,
pleasing style and artfully arranged in handpainted saucers
and bowls. After a few sips of the tea I felt more relaxed,
and I found myself profoundly at ease in this environment
with these two lovely people. Everything seemed com-
pletely acceptable and enjoyable.

We engaged in stimulating conversation throughout
the meal. Mathias told a delightful story of his adventure
in a small coastal town with a seal pup that had become
separated from its mother. The pup could not figure out
how to navigate himself out of a small tidal pool that was
surrounded by high formations of rock, and the mother seal
was naturally cautious about approaching the public shore.
Mathias had struggled with great grunts and groans to re-
unite the two of them by shoving and pointing the pup in
the right direction. His overly animated style and comical
replay of the strategy he used to reunite mother and pup
sent us reeling with laughter until tears streamed out of the
corners of our eyes.

As our laughter quieted, Lola looked at me with
peaceful concern. "It is a great honor for you to be here.
You are one of the most powerful people on the planet.

This is a great day, and you have come a long way to meet with Divine Mother. She awaits you. Because of your important position, you can initiate tremendous change in the world condition."

"Then you know who I am?" I set my teacup down after I had gulped the last amount.

"Of course! We have been waiting for the right opportunity to bring you here. Proper timing was a crucial element. All the circumstances had to be perfect. You had to be prepared and ready for this event, or you would not have been convinced to come. You would have ignored Mathias and simply passed him off as a child playing a silly game. It was a gamble and we succeeded!" Lola hid her smile behind her cup as she took a sip of tea.

"There is still so much I don't understand. I'm not even sure why I followed Mathias to this place. Nothing has made sense to me since I woke up in the hospital this morning. It's highly likely that I have lost all sensibility, and it may well be appropriate to decree the President of the United States insane." The flippancy with which I delivered that line surprised and amused even me.

"I find it amusing as well, and I see it as a good sign. I do believe that you are lightening up, Clarion." Lola chuckled softly and Mathias smiled.

"Do you also read my thoughts as Mathias seems to do?" I queried, feeling quite vulnerable.

"It's more like empathic sensitivity. I feel your thoughts. I feel the vibrational patterns of your thinking. I felt your amusement just now. Earlier, during prayer, I could feel your confusion and apprehension. When one becomes more accepting and non-judgmental; when the heart center opens to love, compassion and understanding; when one is able to live in the moment and give selfless service to others, then the capacity to be empathic and telepathic develops automatically. Everyone has this ability. However, not everyone chooses to develop this side of human nature." She took another sip before quietly setting the cup on the table.

"Why would anyone not choose to develop this ability? If everyone developed this ability it would certainly put an end to unscrupulous behavior. No one would be able hide anything from anyone. There would be no more need for costly protection, law enforcement and punishment systems. I believe that world peace would come about more rapidly. It would put an end to the old institutions that are based on doubt, fear and mistrust. World transformation could happen if we chose to develope this capacity." I recalled similar words which my daughter had enthusiastically spoken on this same matter.

"People choose not to develop this side of their nature because they continue to be fearful and full of self-doubt." Lola became a bit serious as she went on, "When one does not accept himself or lacks self-appreciation, one has a tendency to hide behind pretense and lies. When one is dishonest or has doubt about himself, he causes the human energy field, the aura that surrounds and penetrates the body, to contract. The contraction actually interrupts and depletes the flow of life-force energy. The contracted auric field of that person is a little weaker. That is why sensitive lie-detection equipment works so well. The e-quipment detects a shift or fluctuation in the electrical current of the human energy field. Lying, doubt or dishon-esty causes a condition similar to a short circuit. The human energy field, which is electro-magnetic in nature, falters enough in its flow to register a response on the sensitive equipment. A sensitive individual, an empath, is able to detect this shift in the human energy field as well, often with far greater accuracy.

"And so when the human energy field contracts through dishonest or doubtful behavior, it is much more difficult to develop telepathy and telempathy simply because contraction generates a wall that keeps telepathic information from being felt or interpreted appropriately. However, one who is open, centered, honest and authentic will become highly developed in his ability to know another's thoughts and feelings."

I contemplated her words briefly and asked, "What would you say about someone who lies to protect someone else? There have been countless situations where hiding the truth has saved precious lives. Certainly there are special circumstances where lying is acceptable."

Lola looked quietly to the far side of the room and out into the garden. She seemed to be transfixed on something out there when she responded. "Intention is the key. The intention that a person has when he chooses to avoid telling the truth makes an important difference. If a person lies to bolster a false image of himself to impress others, then it is obvious that this is life-force depleting. If one lies to protect his own image for personal gain and others are harmed or discredited in some way because of his lies, this too causes life-force depletion. When one finds himself telling a lie because his soul intention is to protect or serve another for a higher purpose, then this is quite another matter. In that event it is never for personal gain, and the life-force energy is not depleted."

Looking down at my empty bowl, my mind raced to those times in my life when I had lied and put up a false image to avoid exposing my weaknesses and faults. For fear of appearing stupid or inadequate, I lied and got away with it many times. Yet as I grew older, the importance of telling the truth became crucial. I felt more empowered and happy with myself when I was honest, even when being honest meant facing some humility because of mistakes that I had made.

"People have put their faith and trust in me over the

years because I tell the truth." Speaking slowly and de-
liberately, I went on, "I feel good about myself when I am
honest and authentic. I guess you could say that I take
responsibility for my conduct. I believe what you say
about life-force energy. I feel better and stronger when
I tell the truth. And telling the truth encourages others to
put their trust in me."

"Trust! Now there's a subject which we could talk
about for a long time. Trust is something you are going
to learn a lot about on this journey. And so, it's time for
you to meet the Divine Mother. You must be tested before
you set foot on the path that takes you into the forest."
Lola gathered the bowls and saucers in a hurry, stacking
them neatly on the tray, and scurried out of the room with
the load.

"Why do I have to be tested, Mathias? What's going
to happen?" I whispered, bending close to him and realiz-
ing that I may not get an answer that makes any sense
considering the series of events so far.

"You need to be in the right state of mind and
attitude before you go into the most sacred place of all.
The test will tell us if you can survive your visit with
Divine Mother." Mathias answered casually.

Survive? What does he mean by survive? What
greater trouble could I be getting myself into by having a
conversation with an interesting woman? My thoughts
were interrupted when Lola returned and gestured for us to
move out into the garden.

FOUR

The scent of roses and unfamiliar fragrances filled the air, and I felt lighthearted and eager. We strode upon a wooden walkway and out through an opening in a high, well-trimmed hedge. Spread out before us, on a vibrant, green carpet of grass, was a beautiful array of statuary, so arranged as to lead one's eyes toward a magnificent central figure. This alabaster sculpture was larger than life and nearly translucent. I stood there, gazing at it in awe.

Speechless, I looked at Lola as she returned an understanding nod. She motioned for us to join her on a white marble bench stationed in front of the towering form. As we sat in silence, I studied the fine lines and delicate clefts of this extraordinary sculpture: a beautiful, serene woman with arms slightly outstretched. The palms of her hands faced outward as if she were about to embrace someone. Her intricately carved robe flowed gracefully from the top of her head, cascaded softly about her face and shoulders, then fell downward into gentle folds to her bare feet, which rested upon the crescent moon and a cluster of stars. The figure reminded me in many ways of renditions of the image of Mother Mary; yet the exquisite detail of this brilliant sculpture far surpassed anything that I had ever seen. As my gaze lingered on the face, it seemed that her eyes scanned my soul as if in search of my intention. I removed the Mother Mary pin from my sweater and was astonished to discover that the small figure on the pin was an exact scaled-down version of the sculpture. I glanced at the large, white figure and back to the pin several times to make sure that the pin was, indeed, a representation of the statue before me. I turned toward Lola to announce my discovery, but she held her finger to her lips to hush any intrusion on the silence. Reluctantly, I complied and put the pin into my pocket.

We sat for many minutes, Mathias with eyes closed and hands folded in his lap, while Lola did the same. Closing my eyes, I decided to join them.

As the silence deepened, I became restless and uncomfortable. Then I remembered what Mathias had said to me earlier in the day about finding that quiet place within me. I decided to quiet my mind and listen . . . for what, I was not yet sure.

As a tingling sensation began to envelop me, I became nervous. I attempted to relieve my anxiety by taking some deep, slow breaths, but the sensation increased, as did my heart rate. Then, a vaguely discernible voice whispered softly inside my head.

"Be not afraid, Clarion. Have good faith. Trust in me for I have much to tell you."

Startled by the voice, I opened my eyes, only to find that Mathias and Lola were sitting calmly beside me, their eyes closed as if nothing had happened.

I opened my mouth to speak, only to stop myself. Obviously, they were not at all disturbed. So I closed my eyes again, and dared to deepen my experience. As I regained a more peaceful state, the sensation returned. This time I chose to remain calm and receptive while focusing only on my breathing.

The voice spoke again with greater clarity, "You are doing well, Clarion. I come in love and with the deepest concern for all of humanity. Do not fear me. The sensation that you feel is the emanation of my divine love, compassion, and the life-force energy that it generates. Allow yourself to be at ease with this power before you meet with me in the forest. Do not let your fear overwhelm and control you. Do not let it stop you from receiving my love. You will not perish; you will not be harmed. You will be renewed and strengthened through my love, and through the knowledge and wisdom that I have to share with you. You must come to understand the importance of your work in this world, not only as the leader of a great country, but also as a guiding spiritual light for others."

Her words were soothing, and a wave of peace washed over me. I felt safe, but what she said made me uncomfortable. Me, a spiritual light that guides others? I don't think so. I am the least likely candidate for a spiritual leader. She will have to find someone who is a great deal more willing and capable than I. I wondered . . . was that really the voice of Divine Mother? *Who are you?,* I asked silently.

There was no answer, only a deep, pleasant peace that embraced me. Relaxing, I basked in this peace for what seemed to be a long time before I opened my eyes to find that Mathias and Lola had been watching me patiently.

"You heard her, didn't you?" Mathias chirped brightly. "You heard Divine Mother! She spoke to you because you were able to be quiet enough inside to listen. You passed the test!"

"Test? Was that really Divine Mother speaking? It was different than listening with my ears when someone talks to me. It was like a conversation somewhere inside my head. I felt a tingling sensation, and my heart beat faster." I scratched my head in wonderment.

"The heart beats faster in response to a higher energy, a higher consciousness," Lola reassured. "To put it simply, Divine Mother lives in a state of unconditional love, and the energy of unconditional love vibrates at a very high frequency. When you allowed yourself to be open to her presence by being quiet and calm enough to listen and receive, her energy blended with your own. The physical body, because it functions at a lower level of consciousness, has a lower vibrational frequency. Her own consciousness, which is higher, has a quickening effect upon the frequency of your body. Your heart beat faster as a response to the higher vibration of her presence.

"Her consciousness emanates pure love, pure compassion — a state that we are not familiar with in this world. Her presence can be most uncomfortable for those who still live in fear, guilt, hatred and doubt. That is why you had to be tested in preparation for your journey into the forest, where she will materialize before you."

My heart raced with excitement at her last remark — or was it fear that spurred my heart into racing? "Do you think I'm really ready for this? Divine Mother seems like one hell of a powerful woman. I wouldn't want to make any stupid mistakes." I gazed upward once more into the eyes of the tall, white figure that seemed to be alive and illuminated from within.

"Do you see that Mathias and I have been harmed in any way?" Lola asked. "I have been communing with Divine Mother for years. Mathias has been receiving her guidance as well. My ability to accept and work with her infinite love and power has enhanced my life beyond my highest aspirations. She has taught me to remember my true nature, my natural self. She has guided me to reconnect with the eternal life-force energy. Would you ever guess that I am ninety-five years old?" Lola tilted her chin upward and raised an eyebrow.

"Ninety-five? That's impossible! You're in your fifties at the very most." I blurted out hoarsely, nearly choking on my surprise.

"Not so, my child," she smiled teasingly. "Do you not look and feel younger than you did yesterday? You have been touched by Divine Mother for sure."

"I have so many questions that my head is about to burst! I need to know about — " I broke off when Lola once again ushered my silence with a mere finger to her lips.

"Not now," she said firmly. "There is something important I must attend to. Please go out and explore the rest of the garden with Mathias and enjoy yourself. I will be back in a short while to send you on the path that will lead you to Divine Mother."

Before I could protest, she vanished through a small gate, leaving me quite frustrated and bewildered. I felt the skin of my face, marveling again at the softer, younger texture. There is so much I don't understand, and so little of this has made any sense to me.

"It's not supposed to make sense when you — "

"I know, I know!" Cutting him off, I remembered Mathias' words about analyzing things too much. Smart kid. "No one here treats me with the respect I deserve as the President of the United States. I've been hushed up, ignored, and coerced. A small boy has succeeded in abducting the most important person in America. Look at me! I'm completely insane, chasing after some illusion. It's got to be a trick, an hallucination. Tell me it's just a dream!"

"Lets go out into another part of the garden," Mathias urged with a wide grin. "It's the perfect time of day to walk along the streams and feed the fish."

"Did you hear anything I just said?" I squinted at him, only to be confronted with that angelic, innocent face.

"I heard you. I guess I want you to have a good time while you're visiting, and not to worry about anything. Everything is being arranged. Divine Mother is watching over you and protecting you. Remember the lapel pin." He turned away, skipping along the stone pathway until he disappeared behind a profusion of rose bushes.

Pulling the lapel pin out of my pocket and pinning it to my sweater, I sighed with a huff and proceeded to follow him.

Along the path, I found myself lingering at various places to appreciate the view. The scene was breathtaking. Countless varieties of splendid flowers spilled over immaculate landscaping in great ocean swells of color. Unfamiliar, exotic species of flowers welcomed me as I strolled alongside a gentle stream, and I eagerly absorbed their beauty. The atmosphere was entirely tranquil, and I appreciated a degree of solitude that I had not felt since talking the oath of office. No real privacy will ever be possible during my term in office. These tranquil gardens offered an opportunity for me to be alone, and I relished the peace of the moment.

A soft, cool breeze blew through the drooping limbs of willow trees, gently swaying their slender branches, while the lowest leaves brushed the emerald green grasses.

I was drawn to sit beside a small waterfall that gurgled cheerfully, seeming to beckon me to come closer. Tiny star-like flowers dotted the edges of the brook, dancing among blades of long, thin greenery. Surrounded by the abundance and vitality of life, I felt compelled to place my palms flat upon the ground, fingers spread wide to let the grasses poke their springy emerald reeds between them.

Then something came, like a rumbling, from deep within the earth— something vast and fathomless. It vibrated up through my hands and arms, bringing a pleasant warmth into my chest. My heart pounded loudly. I could only describe this as vibrant, powerful life-force energy, flowing upward into my body from the earth. It was a glorious feeling. My eyes welled with tears, and I let them fall to the earth as gifts of appreciation. The power of this place was beyond anything I had ever experienced.

A flash of light gained my attention, and when I turned to look at it, a small, gossamer-like creature dissolved right before my eyes! Gasping, I fell back on the grass and scooted away quickly on the seat of my pants. Then I heard muffled laughter. It was Lola, standing behind me among the bushes, with her hand over her mouth as she tried to stifle her glee.

"What's so funny? Did you see what I saw? Did you see it?" Excited, I pointed in the direction of the appearance, but saw nothing unusual. "Something was there. I swear it was there! It looked like a tiny, fragile, human being with wings. I-I c-c-could see right through it." I stammered, continuing to point at nothing. "It had large, dark eyes, pointed ears and wispy hair. It looked right at me, and then just disappeared!"

Lola sat down next to me, still laughing and obviously enjoying the astonished look on my face.

"You saw a deva, a nature spirit. It was only one of the millions of devas that live here. You were quite privileged to see one, and it's always a good sign when you do. It means that you're opening up and beginning to move more into your spiritual-heart center . . . right here." She lightly touched the center of my chest with her fingertips.

Looking around at the trees and shrubs as if searching for something, she pointed to a low limb on a nearby cedar tree. "Look there! See? They are very curious about you."

Squinting my eyes, I looked where she was pointing and saw nothing.

"There! Look there! Don't look with your mind — look with your heart," she directed.

"What do you mean, 'look with my heart'?" I asked,

continuing to stare into the trees.

"Remember what you were doing before you saw the deva?" She blushed slightly as she went on. "Please excuse me for not announcing my presence when I caught up with you. I realized you were in deep communion with the earth and chose to respect your experience by remaining quiet until you were complete with it. You were experiencing a heart connection with the power and spirit of the earth. You were being blessed by her as she returned your appreciation.

"The earth is alive and conscious. She knows when she is being appreciated and always gives back in some beautiful way. The deep connection with the earth moved you into a higher state of vibration and awareness. It opened your heart center and elevated you into a state of bliss, an altered state of consciousness.

"The devas were honored by your appreciation, and they felt the exchange of love. When they came to get a closer look, you were able to see one of them because you were in that altered state of awareness. They are directly nourished through human love, and they thrive on appreciation. They will work closely with a human being when they know they are honored, respected, and loved. The devas flourish here in this magnificent garden, and they enrich the area with vibrancy and health.

"Some species grow only on this land and nowhere else in the world because the devas are appreciated and the earth is loved and cared for. The vitality of the trees, plants, flowers, vegetables, and fruits far surpasses anything that you will find anywhere else. One could create a paradise such as this almost anywhere in the world if the land and all the living things were cherished, nurtured, and revered as sacred.

"When human beings choose to commune with the devas and give them the love and respect they deserve, then the Garden of Eden will be restored to this world." Her face beamed with a special radiance as she gazed into the branches of the trees. "Come now. Try it. Recall the state of awareness you were in just before you saw the deva."

I closed my eyes and focused on my spiritual heart center, where Lola had touched me. I remembered the powerful vibration, the peace, and the welling up of deep feeling. I recalled the gratitude I felt. As I recaptured the experience, my heart began to flutter and my chest became warmer. I smiled and opened my eyes.

There, sitting on the lowest limb of the cedar tree were three little creatures, barely visible. Their big bright eyes twinkled, and little wings on their shoulders shimmered. They snuggled up to each other, and I heard faint laughter like an echo of tiny, tinkling bells. I could hardly believe what I saw, and with that thought, they instantly vanished.

"That was amazing! I actually saw fairies! That's exactly what they looked like to me — fairies from old picture books and stories. They really exist!" A sudden burst of laughter sent me rolling from side to side on the grass. The sight of a grown man thrashing about in such an undignified way spurred Lola on, and we both laughed like carefree, silly children.

"Is this any way for the President of the United States to act?"

I looked up and saw Mathias standing over us, his face screwed oddly into a comical expression. I laughed even harder as the irony of his inquiry struck me. I had not laughed so freely since childhood, and it felt wonderful. Damn the Presidency! I'm having a good time!

Mathias shrugged his shoulders, jumped into the middle of our merriment, and frolicked on the grass beside us. The clamoring of noisy humans must have been quite an entertaining sight for the devas.

Soon, our mirth gave way to a peaceful calm, and we

fell into silence and watched the tops of pine trees as they swayed lazily from side to side in the gentle wind. Fluffy white clouds floated overhead, in vivid contrast to the rich blue of the sky. I felt light and free.

The Presidency, Murphy, the hospital — seemed far away in another time, another reality. This place and this moment seemed more real than anything else. As I sat up and looked around, everything I saw seemed remarkably vivid, sharp and clear, even without my glasses! Maybe I will never need them again. I did not want this day to end. I wanted to stay here forever.

Lola reminded, "It's time for you to get on with your mission. Divine Mother is waiting for you. You have passed the test, Clarion, and you will have a glorious visit with her. You will never be the same again."

Never be the same? I am already changed. I'm certainly not the same person who awoke this morning. I cannot imagine any greater changes than those which have already happened.

We all stood up, brushing ourselves off, and Lola took my hand and grabbed Mathias'. He reached for mine, and as I clasped his little hand, I flashed an extra wide grin in response to his smiling face. We stood silently in our small circle, looking deeply into each others eyes. I never thought that at my age there could still be so much to learn about myself.

"See that path over there?" Lola pointed toward a narrow passage that broke through an area of dense foliage. "Follow it until you come to a large meadow. The path will end there and you will know you are in the right place. Mathias will go with you."

"You're not coming with us?" I asked, feeling quite disappointed.

"I won't be going with you, even though I would

love to enjoy more of your company. However, this is your time with Divine Mother. This is a special event and you must have as few distractions as possible. "She squeezed my hand tightly, kissed me on the cheek, then walked briskly down the path by which she had come.

Remarkable woman, I thought. It's hard to believe that she is so alive at her age. On the other hand, nothing about this day has been as I believed it should be.

Mathias ran to the path that led us to the meadow. He turned, and with a great sweeping gesture called out, "Come on, Clarion! Follow me — it's this way." He ran on with all of the effortless exuberance of an angel in flight, as though he had wings.

"Youth," I muttered, and started up the path. I was being drawn more deeply into this adventure, heading toward a rendezvous with a mysterious woman — and I felt powerless to resist.

FIVE

The forest was heavily clad in shadows of jasper and cool, damp moss. Its floor was covered with decades, even centuries, of fallen trees, which were strewn about and partially hidden among thickets of massive ferns. The sweet songs of birds echoed as they flitted about in search of small crawling and flying things. Stopping occasionally, I observed large beetles that shared the path as a byway to avoid traversing the cluttered ground beneath the trees.

This forest was vitally alive and filled with energy. I could feel that tingling sensation again as I deeply appreciated and revered the life around me.

Although I had not seen any sign of Mathias, I was not worried. He certainly seemed to be able to take care of himself to a great degree. He remained a mystery to me, and so few of my questions had been answered since I arrived here.

The path meandered on until it ended abruptly at the base of an awesome wall of granite rock. I searched for evidence of a continuing path on either side of the rock formation, but saw only dense forest and thicket. There seemed to be no way to move forward other than to climb up the rock. Why didn't Lola tell me about this? It looks to be a difficult climb. If Mathias came this way, how did he manage?

Tilting my head far back, I focused on the summit, but saw no signs of Mathias. Closely examining the surface of the rock, I could see clearly where previous climbers had worn away the stone in various places. Stepping up to the nearest foothold, I began to climb.

The ascent was arduous and exhausting. The higher altitude made it difficult to breathe as I struggled up the face of the granite wall. The rock was at such an incline that much of the time I had to hold my body flat against its surface to keep myself from falling backward. I inched my way up like a crawling insect.

I felt foolish for putting my life on the line again. And for what? How do I know that this whole scenario hasn't been some fantastic conspiracy to eliminate me from the political scene? Could I really trust Lola, Mathias, or someone who calls herself Divine Mother? What about Murphy and the others back at the hospital? What has gone on since I ran out on my presidential responsibilities? Maybe I took the wrong path. What if I have a heart attack? How could I have been so stupid? I stopped climbing, feeling too weary to continue. I must have passed out for a while, and came to when I was startled by the sound of a voice.

"Clarion. Be aware. Pay attention to your thoughts."

I glanced around to see who spoke. Seeing no one, I lay there quietly. Clinging to the rocky wall, I soon realized that I had been doubting, feeling guilty and fearful. I thought of Lola and her assertion that fear and doubt stood in the way of receiving the life-force energy.

Shifting my attention to my heart center, I recalled the joy I felt in the forest when I discovered the devas. I recalled, as well, the peacefulness I experienced while sitting before the sculpted figure of Divine Mother in the garden, and the soothing words she spoke to me.

All the powerful and loving insights I had experienced so far flooded through me, and I felt lighter. As I focused on these things, a surge of energy welled up inside of me and I began to climb once more. Although my strength was renewed, it seemed to be a long time before I reached the top, gasping and perspiring profusely.

Grasping the last boulder, I hoisted myself to level ground. Then, as I crawled the last short distance to safety, I nearly bumped my nose on a pair of familiar-looking shoes. Looking up, I saw Mathias standing there, staring down at my spread-eagle form.

"What took you so long?" he quipped rather flippantly.

"How did you get up here?" I asked, my voice rasping as I struggled to stand up.

"The same way you came up," he stated matter-of-factly, looking fresh and relaxed.

Angrily, I pointed a finger down the side of the huge granite cliff and the path of my very difficult ascent.

"That is one strenuous climb! It's one hell of a dangerous rock to tackle!"

"It is?" Mathias peered over the edge of the rock and was genuinely surprised by my assessment.

Slapping my face with my hand, I knew it would be useless to expect any sensible answer.

"You know, if you try to make any sense of this you'll only — "

"Yes, yes! I know, I know." I sat on a nearby log and buried my face in my hands in supreme frustration. Mathias sat down next to me and patted me gently on the shoulder.

"There, there, Clarion. Things aren't all that bad, are they?" he cajoled softly.

"Why didn't Lola tell me about the dangers on this path? I could have prepared myself. I would have borrowed more appropriate shoes or asked for directions to an

ORACLE OF CLARION

easier route. I'm not a youth like you, Mathias. I have to
be a little more careful." Quite annoyed, I waited for a
reply.

"Well . . . Lola probably didn't think to tell you
about it because there's never been a problem before. And
there is no other way up to the meadow. Besides, you
wouldn't have made the important discovery that you did
while climbing. Why can't you just be happy and grateful
that you made it? You're safe and you're here. There's a lot
to appreciate." Mathias nudged me and pointed to the
horizon.

I looked out at the expansive view that the higher
altitude offered. In the distance, steel blue mountains were
crowned with a rich blanket of bright snow. The closer
foothills were thickly carpeted in dark green piñon and
cedar. Strips and swatches of flowering meadows, deep
ravines, and shimmering streams punctuated the lush
mountain forests. I breathed deeply and came into greater
peace and calm. The day brightened and took on the sur-
real imagery of a brilliant painting. I noticed that I was
very thirsty.

"There's water you can drink from a stream that's
further up ahead. You'll feel better when you start walking
again." He tugged on my sweater, and I drew my arm
around him to give him a gentle squeeze, feeling a little
more at ease with his mind-reading.

Finding the path once more, we followed it into a
deeper part of the timberland and paused by the stream. I
cupped my hands and took many dips into the water before
my thirst was quenched.

Gazing about, I wondered what time it was. I had not
paid attention to the sun's position earlier when we were at
our high vantage point. From within the density of the
forest, it was difficult to tell how much daylight remained.
It seemed as though the day should have given

way to twilight long before now.

We resumed walking, quickening our pace, as the cool dampness of the woods penetrated our clothing. I shivered while Mathias skipped and leaped to keep warm. How cold would it get by evening? Would my visit with Divine Mother be a long one? Would it allow us enough time to descend the mountain before it gets dark?

The farther we walked the more foreboding the forest became, taking on a spooky atmosphere as the woods grew denser and magnificent trees loomed high. The tangle of limbs had woven a heavy canopy overhead, and thick, clingy moss drooped eerily from vines and branches, shutting out the light of the sun.

The birds had stopped singing, and I found the encroaching gloom increasingly disturbing. Mathias drew himself close to me and took my hand. Finding our way through these woods at night without a light would be difficult, not to mention the descent on that granite wall. I felt foolish again, chastising myself for being thoughtless and naive.

Becoming aware that my thoughts were getting the better of me, I focused again on the loving and peaceful energies of my heart center. My doubts and worries began to disappear. As I consciously changed my perspective to one of appreciation and gratitude, I felt the return of the tingling sensation. At the same moment, I saw a narrow sliver of daylight breaking through the darkness ahead of us.

My feet began to gather speed, seemingly all by themselves, as Mathias raced ahead. The small stream of light grew into a wide opening in the forest, and long, cheerful rays of sunshine poured through the trees. I breathed a sigh of relief, and was grateful as the air became warmer. It was here that the path came to an end.

SIX

I found myself standing at the edge of a vibrant, sunny meadow, greatly appreciating the bright yellow sun as it burned away the remaining shivers of cold. Countless butterflies danced and flitted over the meadow grasses as flashes of brilliant light reflected on their wings. The sound of rushing water indicated that its source was nearby, hidden by tall grasses and an endless display of wild flowers. Mathias scurried about, poking a stick cautiously into curious places, no doubt hoping to find some resident creature.

Sitting down on a large flat boulder, I leaned back to rest, with hands under my head. I must have dozed off; for when I opened my eyes, all I could see was an enormous black beetle, wildly wiggling and dangling its fat, hairy legs an inch from my face.

"Aaaaahhhhgg . . . !" I popped off the rock like a shot of lightning. "Mathias! What are you trying to do? Put that thing down!"

"What's the matter? I thought you might want to appreciate him. I've never seen a beetle so huge and beautiful. Here . . . just hold him for a moment." Gleefully, he shoved the squirming beetle toward me.

Pulling back, I blurted, "Mathias, not now! I don't think I'm ready for that." Blushing, I was embarrassed to be so nervous about a creature I could easily squash with my foot. How could I be so squeamish about a bug when

I have had to face far more difficult and uglier characters in domestic and foreign negotiations?

Mathias grinned impishly, "These beetles won't hurt anyone, you know, especially when you appreciate them. Sometimes they get scared and pee in your hand, but that's about all." He gently set the beetle down and studied it intently as it skittled off into the greenery.

Blowing out a sigh of relief, I chuckled with amusement, and watched Mathias as he squatted to study other crawling creatures. Such a special boy. I admired him so. Young, innocent, curious and enthusiastic about everything!

I knew that I had fallen in love with Mathias. How could anyone not fall in love with such an angelic face and lively spirit? His charisma captivated me, and I found myself a willing follower. I wondered how I could keep in touch with him after this adventure was over.

Taking my seat crosslegged on the flat boulder again, I breathed in deeply and absorbed everything around me. Peace prevailed in this beautiful meadow, and I closed my eyes to focus on my spiritual heart center. The tingling sensation returned, filling and warming me from within. Like a great light inside, it glowed, radiated and expanded.

I struggled with the urge to resist this force and tried to relax. As the energy increased, however, I was fearful that something more powerful than I would overwhelm and control me. My thoughts and feelings of fear fought with the opening trust of my heart. Remembering to breathe deeply, I directed the breath into my heart and into those places of my body where there was tension. I changed my thoughts of doubt into appreciation for the day, and focused on the beauty of this place. I was grateful for the companionship of Mathias and all that I had experienced.

As I looked toward the farthest edge of the meadow,

I was startled by the sight of an unusual structure. Blinking a few times and rubbing my eyes, I looked again. Sure enough, it was there. I knew it wasn't there before. I would have noticed something like that!

"Mathias! Look! Do you see that white structure over there?" I pointed, apprehensive that his answer probably wouldn't make any sense to me.

"That's the temple. Divine Mother sometimes appears there." Mathias spoke in that matter-of-fact tone he often used, much to my frustration.

"It wasn't there before. I know it wasn't. How could I miss something like that?" Studying the unusual structure, I sat dumbfounded.

"It's always been there. You can only see it if your heart is open enough. If you didn't see it before, you just weren't open enough to see it. Let's go over there now. Divine Mother is ready to show up." He skipped off briskly towards the structure — the temple, as he called it — and I reluctantly followed, shaking my head in disbelief.

As we drew nearer to the base of the steps which led up to a wide, circular platform, the energy and tingling sensation increased and became quite intense. It emanated from the temple itself. I stopped short, and carefully surveyed the architecture. The exterior of the temple was cylindrical in shape. It towered almost to the tops of the trees, which offered a contrasting backdrop for the temple's opalescent radiance. Twelve bright alabaster columns reached upwards from the edge of the circular floor, supporting a golden dome that glistened in the sunlight. There were no windows or walls, only the broad, airy openess that suggested communion with all of nature and with the life that surrounded the temple.

Twelve steps led up to to the circular platform, and I moved slowly to the first one to take a better look. Mathias had seated himself on the grass. Truly, the temple generated a comforting sense of holiness and sanctity.

My heart beat faster in anticipation as the tingling sensation increased. The atmosphere all around me began to crackle and buzz with an odd electrical energy. This strange and wonderful energy was also greatly disturbing. I had never felt anything like it before. As the intensity of the energy grew, I felt vulnerable, exposed and uncertain of my safety. Staring at the center of the temple, I was searching for a sign that something or someone was about to appear, when a clear, soft voice spoke behind me.

"What are you searching for?"

Startled, I spun around to confront the intruder, but instead found myself looking into the deep, mysterious blue eyes of a beautiful woman. At that moment, a great wave of peace flooded through me.

Mouth gaping, I stood spell-bound and stared into the endless depth of those eyes for what seemed to be a long while, until she gently pressed again, "What are you searching for?"

Snapping to my senses, I exclaimed, "Forgive me! I realize that I have been staring at you quite rudely. I do apologize. I had no idea that anyone else was in this meadow. Your sudden appearance is a great surprise." I extended my hand to take hers in greeting. She held up her hand to stop me.

"Wait. First, you must answer my question." She smiled brightly as her gaze penetrated me deeply.

I did not know why she refused my hand, but it mattered little as I groped for the answer to her question.

"Well . . . " I began rather cautiously, not knowing how much I could safely reveal to her. "Mathias and I are about to visit with someone and we're waiting for that person to show up." Chuckling nervously, I darted a glance at Mathias, who seemed not the least bit disturbed by the untimely arrival of a nosey, but beautiful stranger. In fact, his face was beaming.

"Yes, I know why you have come. Besides that, what is it specifically that you are searching for?" Once more, she pressed on with a soft intensity.

"You know why we are here?" I wondered if this was another one who could read my thoughts. Shifting about on my feet, I pondered her question more deeply. What *am* I searching for? For what reason have I come all this way, risking my life? Has all of this been merely an attempt to satisfy my curiousity about some remarkable woman? What *is* my intention?

I thought for a long time and replied carefully, "I believe that what I am searching for is hope . . . " I paused to gather the full meaning of this realization. " . . . hope for this world, and for all of humanity. One person alone cannot change the world. But, if I could be more effective in the world by gaining new insight, revelation, new knowledge and the wisdom to use it . . . I could share it with the world. Perhaps new insight and knowledge would help to pull us all out of a very difficult and dismal world condition. I would like to believe in the concept of world transformation, as I've heard my daughter and a few other lofty souls talk about so freely. Even though I have rejected the idea of world transformation as an absurd and unrealistic fantasy, another part of me yearns for such a possibility."

I paused, choosing my next words carefully as I went on, "There has been a miracle in my life . . . " Reflecting upon the events that began in the morning, " . . . something wonderful has happened and I have no practical explanation of it. What has occurred on this day defies anything that one could call logic or common sense." As I spoke, Mathias returned a knowing grin.

Looking at the woman before me, I amazed myself, by unabashedly spilling out the entire story.

I began with the assassination attempt, my miraculous recovery, meeting Mathias, the lapel pin, the journey, Divine Mother, the insights, lessons and so on. As my story climaxed with the present, I took in a deep breath and let out a sigh.

" . . . and now here we are, waiting for the appearance of Divine Mother. Based on what I have experienced and learned on this day, I feel as though she may have some very significant answers to some very important questions. Believe my story or not— that's for you to decide. I'm not even sure why I've told you all of this, for you may think that I've spun an impossible tale."

Studying the soft face of this intriguing woman, I thought I saw a fleeting glimmer of amusement, though her look was not unkind. It was as if she knew some secret irony.

"You have been most patient in listening to my story. Now may I know something about yourself?" Eagerly inquiring further, I asked "What is your name and where are you from?"

There was a silence that seemed to suspend the movement of time, as the three of us stood in that splendid meadow. The pleasant warmth and brightness of the sun splashed about our heads and shoulders, and it felt as though I was being bathed in far more than normal sunlight.

The tingling sensation that had become so intense had subsided into an immensely pleasurable feeling of peace and well-being. In the presence of this unusual woman, I experienced a calm that was new to me. Her eyes expressed an ageless wisdom and a mysterious otherworldly demeanor. A flash of sparkling light glittered and danced in her eyes, and I found myself smiling broadly, transfixed by her face.

She spoke softly at first, "I am known by many names ." Pausing thoughtfully, she slowly spoke again, the sound of her voice rising towards a crescendo.

"I have been known throughout the ages as the Great Mother of all creation. I am Isis. I am Asheera. I am Inanna. I am Quan Yin. I am Sophia. I am Mother Mary. I am the Divine Mother. I am Gaia, Nature and Soul of the Earth. I am the Goddess of God. I am the feminine spirit which dwells in all forms, in all men, and in all women. I have come to give hope and healing to all of humanity, to all of the world through the omnipotent power of everlasting love."

So powerful was her delivery of these words that I swooned to the reverberation of sacred names. A river of rumbling sound thundered through every cell of my body. Every molecule of my being seemed to quiver and quake uncontrollably. What was happening to me? I was spinning, losing consciousness. Where was I?

I lost sight of the meadow, Mathias, and the strange woman. I now knew her to be the Divine Mother, and the power she wielded was frightening. Buffeted about in a vortex of crackling energy, wind and light, it seemed as if I was spinning out of control. I shouted for help, and her crisp, clear voice broke through.

"Clarion! Be not afraid. It is the omnipotent power of life-force energy. You are resisting it. Surrender, Clarion. Let go of your need to be in control. Trust is the key. Trust in the innate wisdom of your own soul!"

I did not fully understand her words. Instead, I struggled to force my fearful thoughts into thoughts of gratitude. The spinning and swirling seemed endless as startling blasts of electrically charged wind nearly deafened me. I reached out frantically for something to grasp. Was I upright or was I upside down? I could not tell. I could not open my eyes!

"Cease struggling, Clarion! It's not about controlling or forcing. It's about surrender. It's about creating a

calm mind and an open heart. Let go and learn to allow!
Let go of your need to control. Find that place of peace and
calm within!" she commanded firmly.

Surrendering seemed like the last thing I wanted to
do. Doesn't surrender mean to yield to another's power?
Doesn't it mean to give up? If I surrender, will I be com-
pletely consumed or severely injured by this terrible force?
Or worse, will I die? I panicked as nausea overcame me.

"Surrendering is allowing yourself to be completely
at one with the Divine Creative Force. It means to be at one
with the center and core of your being, which is your
eternal connection with the Divine. When you are centered,
you are residing within the eternal realm of peace and
calm. It's much like being in the still place within the eye
of a hurricane. Find your center of peace and calm within,
Clarion. Trust in the heart-mind and soul center of your
being, which is your infinite oneness with Spirit."

Gathering courage, I relaxed my body as thoughts
of terror emptied from my mind. Breathing more slowly,
I searched for something that could be called the soul
center of my being. I was drawn to the spiritual-heart
center as Lola had shown me, and as I focused my at-
tention on the peace that I found there, the over-powering
force began to ebb.

Latching onto this peacefulness and directing my
focus toward it, I felt a sinking sensation as if I were
falling. I contracted again in fear and the spinning re-
sumed its turbulence. Relaxing once more, I was deter-
mined to move through my fear, to remain calm and open to
a new level of trust within myself. The spinning stopped,
as did the sensation of falling, and I drifted tranquilly in a
remarkable state of calm. Blissful and grateful, I opened
my eyes and was shocked at what I saw.

"No! It can't be!" I shrieked, terrified at the sight
before me. Clapping my hands over my eyes I cringed,

afraid to open them. I peeked through a slit between my fingers. "Oh, no! I can't believe my eyes," and shut them tight again, while I shuddered in disbelief.

"Clarion," the voice of Divine Mother spoke. "You are safe! Open your eyes in wonder and awe. Open your eyes and behold the glorious scene of creation. Be not afraid! Accept this gift and you shall be transformed."

"Do I have to go through *this* to be transformed?" Groaning, I felt my heart pounding as if it would leap out of my throat. Squinting cautiously out of one eye and then the other I exclaimed, "This can't be real! This can't be what I think it is!"

Suspended and weightless, I floated high above the earth, so high that I could see the entire sphere within the scope of my vision. She hung majestically in an endless black velvet sea that was permeated with the glimmer of trillions of stars that blazed like the finest of diamonds. The moon hovered in eerie silence beyond the curvature of the planet, its lonely surface relecting the light of the sun. Pearlescent clouds swirled over azure blue oceans and green and golden brown lands. The whole world seemed illuminated from within, and it was breathtaking!

The incredible scene was so overpowering, so unbelievable that I could not speak. I could not even cry out for fear of falling to the earth! After all, isn't that how gravity works?

"You will not fall, Clarion. You are safe. The pull of gravity is not the same in this place. Compose yourself. Move your attention once more into your soul center, your spiritual heart, and look upon the earth again." Her encouragement was so soothing that I fell into instant trust and focused my attention within while closing my eyes.

The pounding of my heart faded as my breathing became easier than I ever remembered it to be. Of course!

Since I was beyond the usual pull of gravity, the labor of breathing would not be as it was on earth. Come to think of it, why am I able to breathe out here?

"Trying to figure it all out with your mind will only ruin your experience of something beautiful and wonderful," a familiar voice spoke.

"Mathias, is that you?" I opened my eyes toward the direction of the voice, only to find Mathias rotating wildly in an effortless somersault and then a few backflips in space. He spread his arms out high above his head and thrust them downward several times, like flapping wings, and "flew" over to me. He dipped over my head until he parked upside down with our faces only inches apart.

"Mathias! I can't look at you upside down like that. It's making me queasy!" Grimacing painfully and clutching my stomach, I hoped to stop the fluttering. "Please face me in a normal upright position!"

"What's a normal upright position? There is no up or down in space. You're just experiencing your own beliefs of how you think things are supposed to be, and that's not how things are. How do you know that it's not *you* who is upside down and *I'm* the one who is right side up?" He giggled gleefully and tapped me playfully on the nose.

Exasperated, I closed my eyes for fear that the nausea would worsen. Then a gross thought struck me. If there is less gravity, where would the contents of my stomach go if I should give in to vomiting?

"Remember. Stay in your center, Clarion." Divine Mother delivered her words with gentle urgency. "Trust is the key. Trust! You are about to learn many things that will change your life and how you perceive the world condition. Believe that you have the ability to perceive life events in an entirely different way. You must learn to shift your perception from fear to love." She was persistent with her coaching to move me beyond my limited view of life. "You must understand that you are struggling with beliefs which have nothing to do with the absolute Truth! You are struggling with beliefs that are a result of mass conscious-ness conditioning, old beliefs that are based on fear, doubt and misunderstandings that have controlled humanity for many millenniums!"

I thoughtfully considered her words about old be-lief systems while I continued to breathe myself into calm-ness. Old conditioning and programming— we were all influenced by fearful and limiting beliefs, and conditions the moment we were born into the world. These beliefs with their foundation in fear, doubt and misunderstanding have been passed down from generation to generation for thousands and thousands of years. Each family, each cul-ture and even each nation has had their own interpretations and definition of life events.

We have all created our personal beliefs based upon the opinions of others and their beliefs about what they think and believe to be true! Few of us born into the world have ever been encouraged to believe and trust in our individual inner truth and wisdom.

We have, instead, given up our power of inner knowing to others, believing that others know more about us than we know ourselves! We have become controlled and disempowered by giving up our ability to know what is true for us. Although I was well aware of how we become conditioned and molded through the beliefs and opinions of families and societies, I had never before considered these things so deeply.

"Clarion!" Divine Mother coaxed again. The inten-sity of her voice shattered my deep thought. "Will you now choose to look upon the world through different eyes? Can you choose to perceive this situation as something entirely different from what you think it is? Are you willing to change your perception based upon the love, understanding and wisdom that you have in your own heart?

"You can still choose to believe that this is an awful situation, and have all of the reactions of a person who chooses fear and misunderstanding as a response to an experience. Or you can choose to perceive this as an opportunity to discover more about yourself and the world. You can choose to perceive this as a gift of insight rather than a terrible event. It's up to you!"

This was certainly far more than I had ever expected! I never thought that I would be participating in a living nightmare. And yet, is it really a nightmare, or is it an opportunity, as Divine Mother said, to experience something wonderful? Can I move through my fear and into trust? I placed my attention on my spiritual heart-mind, the soul center of my being. Choosing to breathe slowly and relaxing with each breath, I finally felt calm enough to peek out through squinted eyes.

SEVEN

There she was! The magnificent earth still shone in the reflected light of the sun. Looming and majestic, she seemed like a deity that commanded eternal respect. I quietly acknowledged the reverence and awe that surged through me. Hanging in space, I breathed in a rhythm that imitated the gentle rise and fall of the sea, and began to study the outline of continents where land ended, and oceans and enormous inland waters began.

From this point high above the earth, I realized that I was hovering over an upside down North America! Swallowing hard, I felt the queasiness arise once more. Recapturing the calmness of my heart center, I was amused to discover that I, and billions of other earthlings, had been convinced through history books and geographical layouts that the United States was near the top of the globe, the North Pole being "up" and the South Pole being "down."

Even the highly publicized photos taken during our extensive space rendezvous in recent years were "thoughtfully" adjusted so that the continents appeared in the "appropriate" positions, showing the North Pole at the top of the photograph, the United States directly below Canada. The sole purpose was to eliminate any doubt that the planet being observed was, indeed, the earth. What a joke!

My eyes growing wide with awe, I felt something else emerging from deep within. A profound laughter erupted from the depth of my belly and I exploded in tears of joy. The irony of it all! The beauty of it all! This is so fabulous!

Jubilant, I was laughing and crying at the same time. Mathias joined in with the cascade of laughter as he dipped his head to his knees and spun forward into a triple somersault. I imitated his move and discovered the effortless gyration of my gravity-free body. The freedom of movement was so marvelous that I continued with other daring "aerobatics," swooping and spiraling like a cosmic dancer in a grand space ballet.

As my laughter turned to quiet bliss, I faced the earth and beamed to her my deepest appreciation. New tears welled up, tears of yearning. I cared for this great earth. She was beautiful and magical. I loved her, and with this awareness I felt an ache in my heart, as though pining away for a long lost lover.

My eyes scanned the globe that had no boundary lines, no separation of nations, no names of cities nor lines of longitude or latitude emblazoned upon her. From this vantage point, it was easy to imagine a world of freedom for all: freedom to travel anywhere unimpeded; freedom to meet with, to be friends with and commune with peoples of all nations; freedom to be one world and one people. I sighed a deep sigh of longing for that utopian dream.

"Its not just a dream, Clarion." It was the strong, sweet voice of Divine Mother. "The world is ready for transformation. Humanity is ready to evolve into a mighty race that will demonstrate remarkable abilities and will move beyond the present limitations of fear, hatred, doubt, and shame."

As she continued, she spoke more slowly and deliberately. "This is a critical time. Humanity stands at the crossroads of change. Humanity will either choose the way of love, peace, freedom and thus create the utopia of your dreams; or humanity will bring about its own destruction by continuing to wallow in blame, violence, and the control and manipulation of others. It is a matter of *choice*, Clarion. Which path will each person choose to take? Which path will all of humanity take? Will each person choose to take the path that leads to greater love, compassion, understanding, peace, freedom, sharing, service to one another, and everlasting life? Or will each person remain on the path that keeps him in fear, doubt, shame, self-centered behavior, needless suffering and death?"

Her words haunted me as I gazed upon the earth. Could humanity choose love over fear, guilt and shame? How can this transformation take place? It seemed so unlikely that this could ever happen. There was still war, starvation and greed. Even though most nations had agreed to disarmament after the turn of the century, there were still many among the smaller countries whose infantile governments touted their ability to use nuclear weapons. It was a stressful situation for the more mature nations, much like that of a frustrated older brother attempting to reason with an unruly child waving a loaded gun.

What about starvation? So many people still go to sleep hungry. Many new programs, launched in recent years quelled the dire need for food in many countries. People who had been starving were becoming increasingly self-sufficient and sustaining. It had been a long and arduous task to persuade the governments of these countries to change their policies toward their own people. Most of this change of attitude had occurred as a result of boycotts, by the United States and other concerned nations, of specific items exported by these countries.

The promise of money or the withholding of it continued to carry enormously persuasive bargaining power. However, as the worldwide electronic credit became the established medium of exchange, "money" was now easily

71

traced in its usage. The old currency was rapidly disappearing, since the manufacture of coins and paper money ended in the early years of the new century, and had become collectors' items. The new electronic "money" system made it more difficult for foreign governments to abuse any monetary aid given to assist their people in accomplishing a self-sustaining order.

Greed. Greed still prevailed unabashed in most places. People hoarded things, hanging on to useless, old wornout possessions. Competition among families, friends and corporations encouraged accumulation and overspending. The campaign to promote simplicity in America had been difficult, but very effective. Humanitarian strategies encouraged people in all sectors of society to move toward less consumption, to recycle, to share with others less fortunate and to give away those possessions that were no longer being used. Millions of Americans, Europeans, Canadians and Australians supported the movement and enjoyed the simpler life-style that resulted.

Added benefits for these people included the increase in energy and physical well-being achieved through their conscious participation in the dismantling of an extremely materialistic world. Nevertheless, there were all too many who would not give up the old ways, believing that their possessions and the amount of money they could spend gave them security and power, as well as a sense of success. They refused to believe that their actions or refusal to participate in this movement could create unhealthy consequences for someone else. These were the people who continued to indulge the hungry industrial monster of a materialistic culture.

The more deeply I thought about these world dilemmas, the sharper the images became. All at once I realized that I had been moving closely over the land, and whenever I thought of a specific world condition, I was instantly transported to that place without any sensation of travel-ing. I was mesmerized as dramatic vignettes of various cultures projected themselves vividly across my field of vision. I could see everything quite distinctly; in fact, it was almost too realistic, since it made the dire world condition disturbingly real.

I began to think more intensely about the wars which prevailed in certain places on the planet; and in an abrupt flash, I found myself standing on a battleground, surrounded on every side by smothering smoke, blazing fires, and deafening noise. There were shouts and screams of horror as repeated explosions violently rocked the earth.

Terrified, I ran and hid behind a small mound of sand bags. The air was thick with the smell of sulphur and burning flesh. Visibility disintegrated as the choking haze and dust increased, blocking out the light of the sun. I could see no one and heard only the voices of alarm and panic. Small clearings appeared, only to vanish quickly in the thickening walls of smoke. I caught a fleeting glimpse of the dim silhouettes of soldiers as they crouched behind low piles of dirt.

I was afraid, for I did not know if these were friends or foes of Americans. But what did it matter any way? It's so confusing and terrifying here that most would shoot first and ask questions later!

The incredible noise pounded inside my head. Why? Why this insanity? It's truly hell on earth! I caught sight of dead bodies, twisted and lying scattered about. Who were these people? What country was this? As I strained with these thoughts, a soldier seemed to materialize right out of the dingy air. He leaped over the small barricade of sand bags and squatted low, next to me. Scanning me quickly, his eyes wide with panic, he shouted something to me in a language I did not understand. Fading daylight and the dirt and grime on his face made it difficult to guess his nationality. He struggled with his weapon as though it were jammed, and blood trickled down his forehead from underneath his helmet. I examined his uniform for some identification and could find nothing familiar on the battered and dirty clothing. The darkness of evening was fast approaching, even as the intense thundering and pounding of heavy artillery escalated.

The soldier stared into the thickening smoke, having given up on his weapon. He was just as frightened as I was. I shouted out a greeting, trying various languages in an attempt to discover his origin. "Good afternoon" and "Good morning" were all I could remember of any language, and he only glared at me. I could tell by the wild, confused look on his face that he thought I was crazy.

He grabbed my arm, shaking me violently while screaming unknown words into my face; a spray of saliva punctuated each sharp remark. Had I spoken the wrong language in greeting? Maybe he thought I was the enemy. What was I in for now?

He shoved me against the sandbags, resumed his surveillance of the area and ignored me. What was going on in his mind? If only I could understand him. If only I could understand this whole crazy situation! Instantly, I recalled the place I had just come from. Hadn't I been hovering above the earth with Mathias a short while ago? Hadn't I been conversing with Divine Mother? In all of this noise, confusion, and terror, I had completely forgotten about her. I had forgotten all that I had heard and learned. Could all of this be a dream within a dream?

Paying closer attention to my thoughts, I focused once more on my spiritual heart, my heart-soul center. I began to slow my breathing, to relax as much as possible, and to search for something to appreciate. Something to appreciate? How insane! In this hell-on-earth, how could anyone find anything to be grateful for? How could anyone find love and peace? Surely this is where Divine Mother's philosophies don't work. I fell into confusion and despair — it all seemed so hopeless. All of this craziness started this morning. Could so much happen in one day, and was it really happening at all?

"Clarion, I am here!" Divine Mother's words brought welcome relief, and at last I found something to be grateful for. "I am always here for you, if you will choose to listen and not give in to despair. I am with you. Even in this unlikely place you will find love and peace. Remember the eye of the hurricane. You can achieve stillness and clarity within, no matter where you are, no matter what the conditions."

I thought about her words and shook my head in disbelief. Although it was comforting to be reassured, I felt that her outlook was wrong. On this battlefield, people are being slaughtered. Even if these soldiers should escape death or physical harm, war victims were often emotionally and mentally wounded for the rest of their lives! And for what? A piece of land, a few buildings, dwindling resources, money, power and control — a sad state of affairs.

At least I was still alive — that was one thing I could appreciate. But for how long? I watched the soldier as he looked out over the low wall of our protective barrier. I wondered about him. Focusing more intently on the center of my spiritual heart, I was surprised to find myself becoming calmer, and the surrounding chaos began having less of an effect on me.

As I achieved a deeper communion with that peaceful place within me, I heard a voice. It was not Divine Mother, but someone else who spoke inside my head. It was the voice of a frightened man, and he yearned for his wife and two small children. He was grieving painfully, and I was touched with sadness for him, whoever and wherever he was.

In the dim daylight that remained, I watched as the soldier reached up to wipe the tears from his face. I knew he had not spoken a word. He had not moved his lips. Yet this voice inside my head was speaking in a language I could understand. Was I hearing his thoughts? I kept silent and still. The deafening roar of the hellish atmosphere faded into the background while the voice in my head grew louder.

The voice continued to speak, and I learned that this man dearly loved his family. He believed that it was his duty to protect his country from a monstrous enemy that could destroy the homeland and the people he cherished. He longed for peace, and he feared his death. His deep sobbing penetrated my awareness, and I found his suffering almost unbearable. He cursed the war and the prevailing military and government authorities. He cursed the enemy. He called out to God— his version of God— and begged for deliverance. Knowing that God was on his side and the side of his country, he felt certain that He would destroy the enemy.

I could feel his fear rise as the dissonance of awful noise amplified; he knew he was about to die.

The soldier howled in agony, slapping his hands over his ears and knocking his helmet to the ground as he shouted the names of his wife and children. In that instant, an enormous blast struck our tiny barricade, hurling the soldier upward. His arms and head were violently severed from his torso, and I too was catapulted high into the air by the force of the explosion. Cursing, I blamed God for this insanity. How could He allow this to happen? If He was so powerful, why would he let the craziness of war continue? How could He allow an enemy to exist that would kill this man and his beloved family, and threaten his country?

Now I was tumbling over and over within a cloud of white, as though caught within a turbulent ocean wave. Was I dead? Where was I? Was I on my way to heaven or on my way to hell? Surely there was no place worse than that battlefield. I felt tortured and broken as the hideous image of the soldier's dismemberment burned in my memory.

Overcome by confusion, I fell into some unknown void. Fear edged its way into my awareness, and my heart fluttered rapidly. With a soft thud, I suddenly found myself deposited on my rear in a dark, shallow trench with the only light coming from a tiny lantern an arm's reach away. It was nighttime in this unknown place, and I strained to see where I was. Maybe I did end up in hell after all!

At the far end of the trench, something rustled and moved. There was nothing but blackness beyond the light of the lantern, and I froze in terror. If this is hell, with what "thing" could I be sharing this dark and musty place?

Someone struck a match and lit another small lantern. I could see a human hand fumbling with equipment, and when the glow from the lantern reflected upon a face that was quite human, I sighed with momentary relief. The face looked in my direction, and I held my breath.

He spoke in a coarse whisper that seemed questioning, but I did not understand him. He repeated his words in an unknown language, with the tone of his voice becoming more demanding. "Not again," I groaned. "Do I have to go through this again?"

Being fearful about his reaction, I reluctantly and slowly spoke a few words of greeting in various languages. Agitated, he reached for a large metallic object, and when its shaft glimmered in the light of the lattern, I recognized it as a weapon of enormous size. He cocked it with a powerful jerk, and the lump in my throat swelled. Why did I need to go through this? Why was this happening? Where was Divine Mother when she was needed? I want out of here!

In the dull light I could see that he was a soldier, but there was nothing familiar about his uniform that offered identification. Was I in the same battlefield once more? It was quiet, not at all like the hellish nightmare experienced earlier. I reached slowly for the nearest lantern, grasped it and drew it gradually to my face while the soldier aimed the weapon in my direction.

My heart pounded so hard it was almost painful. Please, God, let him see that I am not the enemy. As these thoughts caught my attention, I realized that minutes before I had cursed God and now I was asking for His help. If it wasn't for the danger I was facing, I would have laughed out loud.

As my face became illuminated by the light of the lattern, the soldier's response was one of great surprise. No doubt he was astonished at the sight of a foreigner dressed in civilian clothes, sitting in the trench with him. He relaxed his hold on the weapon and pointed it away from me. Relieved, I hoped that this gesture meant I was safe for the time being. He blurted out a few words in his language, and I could only shake my head and shrug my shoulders in an attempt to communicate my lack of understanding.

All at once, a round of bullets exploded sharply overhead. The soldier doused the light, scrambled to his knees, poked his weapon out of the trench, and returned fire. A torrent of artillery fire whipped through the air with a sudden sweep of earsplitting sound. Clapping my hands over my ears, I shouted and cursed, kicked the lantern, and shattered it into a hundred pieces. Thick blackness consumed us, save for the flashes from rockets and explosions. The thunder of bursting bombs was horrible, engulfing everything around me.

The lone soldier with his pitiful little weapon,

which seemed so huge before, was remarkably dwarfed in comparison to the terrible barrage. Experiencing once more a terrifying situation, I searched for some understanding, some clarity. Thoughts of the previous soldier raced through my mind as I tried desperately to find something to appreciate. But what?

A startling revelation washed over me like a huge wave. Why could I not see this before? The only thing left to appreciate was that place of peaceful centeredness and clarity within me that I was beginning to know and understand: the spiritual heart, the soul center of my being, the God-spark, the God-light within. With this understanding came a great feeling of calm. It spread through my entire being, carrying with it a deep, cosmic feeling of love.

In the midst of all this incredible chaos and danger, I was experiencing love, a level of love that I had never known before. This is truly a miracle! I think I understood what the ancient mystics had long referred to as union with the Divine . . . the mystical experience. I laughed as tears streamed from my eyes. I'm in the eye of the hurricane! I've found it! If this is insanity, I will gladly go crazy.

My ecstasy was interrupted by a man's voice rising up inside my head, and I caught my breath. The soldier had dropped down, squatting low while rummaging in the dark for ammunition. In the frequent flashes and bursts of light I could see his panic, as he searched recklessly through his belongings in the hope of finding more ammunition. He used his last round and fell back against the trench wall, hopeless. He bellowed in anguish and began sobbing. I heard his thoughts as if he were actually speaking.

The tears that had fallen in joy were falling now in sorrow for this man as I listened to his longing for his beloved wife, his children, his home. He cursed the military and the government of his homeland. He once believed that it had been an honor to be a soldier and to protect his country from a monstrous enemy. He realized now that he had given up his whole life, and for what? He called upon his version of God to deliver him, for he knew he was about to die. He was confident that God would destroy the enemy because he knew that He was guiding his beloved nation.

Astounded, I knew immediately that this was the enemy of the previous soldier. I had been deposited in the territory of the enemy, for whom the previous soldier was the deadly opposition. Even though they were opponents, their anguish was the same. Both loved their families dearly and honored their countries. Each believed that the true God was on his side and would destroy the other. These were clearly men who loved deeply, passionately. Yet, they were bitter and hateful enemies toward one another the absurd irony of it all!

I was lost in turbulent waves of thought when a mighty eruption shook the interior of our ready-made grave. Curling up into a tight ball, I prepared for the worst. Another violent blast hit, launching us both into the air. The soldier's body split into more pieces than could be counted. Sickened at the sight, I tumbled limply about within the familiar white cloud, and wondered if my body was split into countless pieces as well? I questioned God over and over, "Why, why, why?"

Brilliant whiteness enveloped me like soft cotton, buffering my tumbling until I came to rest upon what seemed to be a solid cloud, solid enough at least to support my weight. Checking my body for any damage, I was surprised to find not even a scratch! The clouds thinned, and I could see a small clearing just a short distance away from me. In the clearing were two men, engaged in face to face conversation as they sat crosslegged on a surface of billowy white.

I moved toward them, gliding effortlessly upon the cloud. As I neared them I realized that these were the two soldiers of my battlefield experience. Their bodies appeared translucent and were perfectly intact, with no evidence of their violent deaths.

They did not notice me and continued talking. I could understand every word they said. Apparently, in this strange and unknown place, there was no language barrier. As they spoke, each knew that the other had been the enemy only a short while before. They took turns apologizing profusely and mourning over the loss of their loved ones. They shared war stories, and as their conversation continued, they realized how similar their feelings were with regard to their families, their countries, their governments, and the armies in which they served.

Presently, a brilliant, pulsating light appeared over the two soldiers. It hovered momentarily, then descended and gently surrounded them. A peaceful calm transformed their anguished faces, and their bodies relaxed as if in deep relief. The pulsing light took on the form of a human being and in another instant, it was the Divine Mother.

I was so happy to see her and had a myriad of questions to ask. I began to speak, but she held up her hand to stop me. It was clear that she wanted me to witness what was happening with the two men.

She was not visible to them; but her presence initiated a change in their conversation, and they began to talk about their respective religions, with each exchanging his version and idea of God. Each believed that he had the one and only "truth" about God. They argued for a while but stopped abruptly when Divine Mother touched the top of their heads, and then placed her hands over their hearts.

Immediately, they realizated that there was only one God, one Creator, one Loving Supreme Source from which all things in the universe have come. Each man recognized that he loved his wife, his children, his country, no less than the other. Each man understood that the love they experienced was like a tiny drop in the infinite ocean of God's love which permeated everything in creation and dwelled in their hearts like a sparkling jewel of light.

Although humankind had created a variety of laws, rules and beliefs pertaining to God, love was something that could not be contained or limited by any human interpretation. Love prevailed regardless of nationality, color, gender or status. The laws that separated these two men were human-made and were founded upon fearful beliefs and the quest for power and control.

They cried, threw their arms around each other and rocked together like babies. I could feel the energy that emanated from them and knew that a great healing had taken place. I was moved deeply by the scene.

A painful sensation burned in my heart, and at the same time I felt a wonderful warmth and joy. It was difficult to understand. My face was wet with tears as I smiled at Divine Mother. She returned a knowing gaze as wave upon wave of loving radiance washed over me.

"You are feeling the opening and expansion of the spiritual heart within you," she said softly as she went on. "The painful sensation arises from the breaking up of old, hardened and crystallized thought forms caused by beliefs which have kept your heart closed and unyielding in certain life situations. These thought forms have also kept you from developing understanding and compassion. You once carried self-righteous judgements about people who engaged in war. Through this event, you have seen an important truth and have achieved compassion through a new understanding. You have received a beautiful healing.

"These soldiers have received healing as well because they have forgiven each other, and have taken the path of love and compassion instead of fear and hatred. They will be active in bringing about the healing of humanity in their next physical lifetime and will choose the way of non-violence rather than war as a means of creating peace."

Next lifetime? I was familiar with reincarnation, although I had not really explored the prospect of repeating lives in order to learn lessons on how to forgive. I was quite curious about this concept, when she spoke in response to my thoughts.

"You will come to understand more about multiple lives and forgiveness at a later time." Her radiant smile had a curious aspect to it, like that of a child who was up to some mischief. What else could Divine Mother have in store for me? I swallowed hard and tried not to think about it. Instead, I turned my attention to my criticism of those who participated in war. Indeed, I had struggled with those judgements.

The wars in various countries had been a constant, vicious "thorn in the flesh" throughout my term of office. Even though the wars had significantly diminished in their intensity over the last two years, the smaller nations were still quarreling over boundaries and ancient transgressions. It caused unrest in all nations, particularly the United States, since our government was all too frequently asked to do something about it. Do something about it? What? The United States, Japan, Russia, Canada, Australia, all of Europe, and other major nations had agreed to cease sending weapons to these warring countries, although the black market for weapons was continuing to flourish.

Nevertheless, the international arms embargo had been successful in reducing the fighting in those countries and in minimizing threats to more peaceful nations.

My judgments had been unbending toward those

who persisted in the thoughtless slaughter of human be-
ings. I had considered them less than human and unworthy
of respect.

I looked to Divine Mother and asked, "Why is there
still so much bloodshed? Yes, my eyes and heart have
been opened to a deeper understanding, and I am grateful
beyond words. Yet, what about the leaders of these nations,
who want power, money and control at the cost of human
life? As long as these leaders have such great power, most
of their people will do as they are told, believing it is the
only choice that they have. Those who actively protest
these leaders are often put to death. What can be done?
How can anyone have compassion for leaders who dictate
such a fate for their people?"

EIGHT

Divine Mother looked at me longingly, as if I were her only beloved child. Basking in this marvelous love, I soon lost sight of her and found myself sailing close to the earth once more. The ground rose up swiftly to meet me, and suddenly I was hovering over a large, old tree.

As I floated downward, my attention was drawn to a small child playing in the shade below. Silently touching down on a huge limb, I sat on this perch for a while and observed the child, a small boy of four or five, raking his fingers through the dirt as if making roads for his toys. He made sounds like a motor with his lips, adding drama to the landscape that he sculpted. A warm smile crept across my face. His precious innocence reminded me of Mathias and I realized that I missed him. I hoped he was alright, wherever he was.

My enjoyable observation of the child was abruptly broken by the sound of a banging door on a house that was at least a hundred yards away. A big, stocky man strode briskly up to the boy, grabbed him harshly by the arm, and pulled him toward the house. His little feet tripped one over the other, and he fell several times. Then he was dragged on his knees. He cried pitifully as the big man shook him violently and slapped him hard in the face, causing his little head to snap back.

Stunned and enraged, I bellowed at the man, but it

seemed as if he did not hear me. I shouted again to get his attention, and there was no response. He slapped the little boy once more before jerking him into the house and slamming the door behind him.

My body shook with fury as I groped my way down the tree, finally landing clumsily on shaky legs. Marching up to the door, I pounded with my fists, "I am the President of the United States of America! I am making a citizen's arrest. You are abusing a helpless child. Open this door at once!" It dawned on me that I hardly presented a believable image of the President, standing alone and dressed as I was. Nevertheless, I could not let him hurt that child. I beat on the door again, but there was no answer.

Discovering that the door was locked, I ran around the house to the nearest window and peered in. There were others in the house, probably the rest of the family. Seven small children, six of them girls of various ages and a tired looking woman whom I guessed was the mother, were seated around a table in the kitchen area. The boy wept uncontrollably, and a wide cut above his right eye was bleeding. His siblings could only stare at him. They were all terrified of this big man, who must have been the father. He was shouting loudly and stomping back and forth across the floor as the woman calmly went about scooping servings of food onto each plate. I got the impression that she must have been through such tirades with this man many times and had numbed herself to them. The children, of course, had not learned this and were frightened.

I banged on the window but no one looked my way. I heard Divine Mother's whisper inside me, "They can neither hear nor see you. Observe, Clarion. Observe and learn." She said nothing more.

Observe and learn? Just stand here and watch? She must be kidding. I wanted so much to protect that little boy and also wanted that bully of a man to pay for his crimes.

Watching helplessly, I cringed as the woman suddenly came alive and engaged in a hostile argument with the man. Apparently, I was once again in a foreign country, hearing them speak in a language I did not understand.

It was too much for me to bear when the brutal man began to batter his wife viciously. All the children began to scream. The little boy jumped from his chair and pounded his father's legs with his fists. This did not discourage the man from pummeling the boy's mother. Finally annoyed with the nuisance, he kicked his small son across the room.

Doubling up in horror, I sank to my knees and could no longer watch the dreadful scene. It was worse than barbaric, worse than evil. I cried because I could not help him. Once again, I challenged God. Why? How could God allow something like this to happen? Why does Divine Mother want me to witness this and yet be unable to do anything about it?

I rolled over on my side and clutched my stomach. What could I do to save this little boy? He was innocent, helpless. And what of the other children? How long would they have to endure this living nightmare? Closing my eyes, I became dizzy with frustration and disgust. I felt a sense of heaviness come over me, like a great weight pulling me down, and I could no longer stay awake.

When I opened my eyes, I was surprised to see the sun rising over the mountains in the distance and to realize that somehow I had slept through the entire night. Hearing movement inside the house, I leaped to my feet and peeked into the kitchen. It was the man I had seen the night before. Still seething inside, I glared at him and vowed that I would find a way to help that little boy and the other children.

In the bright light of the kitchen, I could see the big man easily. Strangely, he appeared much older than yesterday. His hair was streaked with gray, and he was slightly humped over. Perhaps he strained himself in yesterday's skirmish. There was his wife. She also looked older, miserably older. I knew these were the same people, but what had happened to them?

A young boy of about fourteen or so entered the room with books and papers, most likely preparing to go to school for the day. He sat down at the table for his breakfast and was joined by six other adolescents, all girls. Looking at the boy, I noticed a scar over his right eye, and after surveying all their faces, I realized that these were the same children. Mysteriously, I had been transported to the future! In a panic, I quickly checked my own body for signs of aging, but nothing seemed to have changed. Bewildered, I returned my attention to the children and studied them intently.

The young boy was the same boy I had witnessed being brutally abused as a child. He had fresh injuries on his face. The set of his jaw showed a hostile determination and a silent, dreadful rage. A vacant stare had replaced the precious innocence I had once seen in his eyes.

I turned to look out to the mountains. The sun had climbed higher in the mid-morning sky. Disoriented and confused, I closed my eyes and begged Divine Mother for understanding. What was all this for? What was she trying to show me?

Staring once more into the kitchen, I was greeted with yet another scene. The mother was bent over the stove with her back to the window, and when she turned to wash her hands in the sink, I could clearly see that she had aged even more! She looked beaten and haggard. Her eyes were deep hollows of despair. My heart went out to her, and I wondered why she had not left the bully of a man long ago and taken the children with her.

A young man entered the room, wearing a uniform

similar to those worn by foreign military schools. He was a rigid-looking young man with a foreboding coldness in his eyes, as if he yielded for nothing, for no one.

He sat down at the table and coldly commanded the old woman. I gasped. The little boy was now a young soldier, and what I saw in him was most disturbing. The scar on his forehead remained, and I saw the years of abuse in his eyes, and the hatred that was born of that abuse.

He shrieked at his mother when she did not respond quickly enough. When she turned to reprimand him for his disrespect, he stood up and struck her so sharply across her face that she fell to her knees. She rolled over on her side, moaning and crying. Uncaring, he simply turned away and left the room.

Falling to my knees as well, I could not believe what I had seen. That sweet little boy who once tried to beat on his father to stop him from hurting his mother had himself become a monster. I buried my face in my hands and wept.

When I finally looked up, the scene had changed once more. I was on a military base with huge columns of soldiers marching about. Springing to my feet, I ran for cover, fearing that I might be seen. As I hunched behind the corner of a building, Divine Mother's soft voice reminded me that I could not be seen by these men, and that I was only to observe and learn.

"I'm tired of learning," I protested. "This has been too much for me! Please, can I go home now?"

Loud voices in the building caught my attention, and I tip-toed to the closest window to peek inside. I saw the back of a large man, who was adamantly addressing several military personnel seated in the room. As he spoke, he emphasized his words by beating repeatedly on a desk with his fists. The language was unknown, but the intensity of his words were obviously angry and condemning.

The appearance on the men's faces confirmed the

nature of this man's harsh words. There was not one man in the room who appreared to be at ease. His shouting intensified, reaching an irritating pitch. He grabbed a coffee cup, and smashed it on the desk. Fragments shot out everywhere, startling the men, who jerked in their seats.

He roared at them, gesturing wildly for them to leave the room, and the men scrambled at his command. When the last man disappeared from the room, the large man bent over his desk, leaning heavily on his hands and breathing wearily. As he rose and walked toward the window, I could see him clearly and was astonished to find that this was the young military man that I had watched from the kitchen window! By the look of his profusely decorated uniform, he had achieved a very high rank.

I knew this man! In his maturity, I recognized him as the ruling dictator of one of the present warring countries on the planet. I had just witnessed scenes from his childhood! Gaping, I recalled that his man-become-monster was once a child who meant no harm to anyone, a child who had played happily and innocently under the shade of a large tree a long time ago, just as any child would. He was no different, except that he had endured a horrible childhood. No wonder he was the way he was. He was treating his people, his country, and the world exactly the way he had been treated. Neither respect, nor real love, had ever been experienced within his family. Abusive force and control were the frightening foundations of his world.

How could he appreciate and honor human life when he did not even know what it felt like to be appreciated and honored himself? The look in his eyes was that of one who lived in fear and hate. He had learned to control and abuse others as a way of protecting himself from ever again being controlled or abused by anyone else.

He hated because he did not know what love was. He was abusive because he developed the belief, as a child, that kindness and gentleness were signs of weakness, and were qualities which made him vulnerable to abuse and ridicule from others. He instilled fear in those around him and intimidated them. That was how he learned to maintain his post and his sense of control.

I understood that the power and control he so coldly and tenaciously strived for was a continuing quest to quell the painful emptiness within himself. He lived with the belief that the more power he gained by robbing it from others, the better he would feel about himself, and that it would make the hurt go away. In many ways, he was still the small child, striking out vengefully to gain some payback for all the misery he had endured. How could someone like him be helped? It was only moments before that I vowed to find a way to help him as I watched his father beat him mercilessly when he was just a little boy.

Even though I hated war and had judged the warmongers as less than human, I looked upon this man in a totally new light. His rulership was horribly destructive, cold, and inhuman. I could not, however, let go of the realization that somewhere underneath that monstrous exterior was a little child crying out for help, telling the terrible story of his unhappy childhood, over and over, through the atrocities he committed on others.

I sat down on the ground, dumbfounded with what I had learned. Closing my eyes, I leaned back against the building and breathed deeply. I wanted to feel good again, to be in that beautiful meadow with Mathias and Divine Mother. I wanted to feel that love and peacefulness.

In my mind's eye, I saw a vivid image of the dictator trying to force and manipulate others to love him, only to succeed in causing them to fear him. During his periods of solitude and loneliness, he sometimes allowed a tear to gather in the corner of his eye, for that was the only grief he permitted himself to feel. My heart went out to him in that instant, and I sent him all the compassion I could muster.

I prayed that he would find a way to acknowledge and heal his deep wounds and to learn how to accept himself. I also prayed that through this realization, he might learn that it is a terrible sickness to hurt others intentionally.

Through my inner vision, I saw a tiny glimmer of hope in his eyes, a small spark of light in his heart. Sighing heavily, I wished I could do more. Then the voice of Divine Mother spoke.

"You have found compassion for someone who most sorely needs it. The violent, abusive, and degrading behavior of this man, and others like him, will never end if humanity retaliates with the same violence, abuse, and degradation. To hate this man and others like him is to keep that hate alive. To escalate war in order to bring about peace only creates more war.

"Yes, it is true that the innocent and the powerless need protection from the insane and power-mad bullies of your world. Nevertheless, to try to achieve peace and fairness through the use of abuse and control only serves to nourish violence and oppression, the very activities that you claim you wish to stop." Her voice reverberated throughout my being, bringing shivers of recognition, and I knew that she was right. Divine Mother's words seemed to enfold me in a warm, soothing cocoon of wisdom, and I listened, eyes closed and peaceful, as she continued.

"When you sent this man your compassion, you planted in him a powerful seed of love. Even though, to your way of thinking, it may seem small and inconsequential, that tiny seed of love has influenced his consciousness. It has created a shift in his thinking in certain areas, so that he can view his actions from a higher and more enlightened perspective. This will help lead him toward a broader understanding and will increase the potential for reconciliation of his actions.

"No matter how small the shift may be in comparison to the monstrous attitude of this man, it will still serve as a catalyst for change within him. The immense power of prayer and love can never be overestimated. Humanity has the power to transform the world condition into everlasting peace in a single day if only one third of your population joined together in loving prayer and visualization to bring peace and plenty for all!" Divine Mother's voice thundered, and I trembled with the power of her words.

"Do you mean that praying for peace and visualizing abundance for everyone on the planet can actually have an impact? Are you saying that the prayer I sent to this man has caused some change in him?" I queried, disbelieving.

"Remember, thoughts and feelings have enormous power in your world." She added, "The mind is a powerful tool that focuses and directs the limitless flow of creative life force energy.

"When the mind's ability to discern and to imagine in great detail is coupled with the power of wisdom, compassion, and understanding, then painful life events can be transformed and healed. The mind and the heart blending together in unison creates the Heart-Mind connection. The heart alone, which represents the feeling, higher wisdom and intuitive natures, cannot create the reality you prefer. It needs the directing force of intention, discernment, and focus of the mind. The mind alone, which represents the natures of logic and intellect, cannot create the reality you prefer without the feeling nature, wisdom, limitless love and understanding from the heart.

"Humanity has unconsciously and unknowingly used the power of the mind to create and perpetuate suffering, struggle, and limitation in your world for millenniums. The creative power of the mind has been adversely influenced by doubt, guilt, and fear within the imbalanced emotional nature. Without the power inherent in love, the mind becomes little more than an unfeeling machine, cranking out endless intellectual ideas and opinions that are lifeless and void of passion. Without love, the mind entertains itself with analysis, inappropriate and restrictive judgments, repetitive and unconscious thought patterns and distractions that further overstimulate the mind and intellect. This generates denial and lost awareness of authentic feelings and emotions. It promotes a dry dissociation from the subtle sensitivities of the body, and further separates one from a deeper sense of unity with all of life.

"Without the focus and direction of the mind, love is a source of magnificently wild, ecstatic, passionate emotional energy and creative power, but it is a power that remains scattered, diffused, and ungrounded. This leads to the experience of overwhelming emotions and lack of appropriate discernment and rationality."

Listening intently to her words, I seemed to drift along on a pleasant, quiet river of soft light. I floated peacefully, feeling my strength restored. For the first time, I realized that many of us use the power of our minds to judge others unfairly, without attempting to understand them. It was disturbing to discover that my judgments of others could actually have an impact on them, and could limit them from making progressive changes in their lives. All too frequently we judge our family members and friends unkindly. Our intent in doing this, whether consciously or unconsciously, is to control them and to limit their own perception of who they are and what they are able to do.

I recalled a particular cousin who was born quite sick and weak and remained that way throughout her life. Friends and relatives treated her differently than they treated anyone else and focused a great deal of attention on her weakness. She received pity from all of us. I wonder how much we contributed to keeping her sick through our behavior toward her? How could she ever achieve greater health and well-being if she is surrounded by people who always think of her as sick and unable to take care of herself? This was a startling revelation. Divine Mother went on.

"It is one thing to have compassion for people who are sick or disadvantaged, and to assist and support them when they genuinely need help. It is quite another matter to collude with these more unfortunate ones by focusing attention on their weakness and disabilities rather than on how they can help themselves heal and improve their lives. All of you have friends, family members, and relatives, who need loving support to move beyond their current weakness or life challenge. Instead of pity, criticism or disdain, they need empathy, support, and encouragement to help draw out their fullest potential as human beings.

"Many of you find yourselves in relationship with someone who has had a long-term weakness, imbalance, or troubled condition in life. Many of you do not want these weaker ones to improve their condition of weakness or disadvantage, as this position of inferiority ensures that you are superior. This often provides you a measure of control over them which tilts the balance of power your way. Those of you who have controlling natures will often find that you are attracted to those who are weaker, less functional or less 'together' than you in some way. In your relationship with these individuals, you will strive to remain in control through subtle, indirect forms of behavior. For example, you may disapprove of any acti-vity that might help them grow beyond their limitations; or you may use stronger, less subtle measures, such as frequent criticism or perhaps even physical violence.

"Those who need to be in control will not want others to grow, improve, find happiness or become self-reliant. Those who need to be in control do not want others to transform their life conditions into better situations, for fear that if they do, they may gain more power and more control over them or may even abandon them."

Divine Mother's wisdom brought to my mind all the troubled ones in the world: the city gangs, criminals, murderers, rapists, terrorists, disturbed and insane men and women from all walks of life. What are their stories? What pains do they carry? What deep wounds are they suffering? How many such conditions are amplified and perpetuated by the thoughts and beliefs about them that are held in our mass consciousness? How have we as a society kept people in a state of limitation, powerlessness and control due to our beliefs about gender, race, color, status, and disabilities?

To develop understanding of the more incorrigible ones of our world is certainly not to excuse the abuse and violations these troubled ones have committed. Abuse is abuse, no matter how one chooses to look at it, and abuse in any form must never be tolerated under any circumstance.

But, if we really tried to understand the offender, if we began to educate these troubled people and encourage them to develop honor, respect and belief in themselves, might they, in time, develop honor and respect for others? If they were taught to recognize the Divine spark within themselves as Divine Mother said, might they discover how united they are with all of life?

I had been sitting there, eyes closed, for what seemed like a very long time. As I reflected on all these ideas, and on the words of Divine Mother, a strange sensation rippled through my body. I wondered: Are these ideas far-fetched? Are they really too idealistic, too far removed from what we call reality? Or, are they possbile?

NINE

I opened my eyes and found myself soaring quietly in the night sky, then low over the earth once more. Dipping in and out of crowded cities, I caught glimpses of troubled life in the darkness of trash-laden alleys and old, crumbling, vacant buildings.

Murder and rape nauseated me as scenes of these horrid violations flashed across my vision. Thieves and terrorists ran like scurrying rats through sewer tunnels and concrete washes. I saw the mentally disturbed, alone and abandoned by their families in cold and insensitive mental institutions, hospitals, and street slums. I did not want to see any more, so I called out to Divine Mother. I just wanted to be back in that beautiful meadow. Instead, I was hurled toward a black place in the city, as if I had been shot out of a cannon. As I drew closer, I saw a large gang of teenagers running through a dark alley.

Suddenly, I was running, leaping, dodging with them. My legs were quick and lithe with a youthful vitality that hurtled my body effortlessly over the obstacles in our path. There were others who ran with me through dark, narrow canyons of concrete walls, perforated with hundreds of blackened windows that were like cold staring eyes watching everything without concern.

The night air was thick and sultry. We ran, pausing to hide behind piles of garbage. The eyes of my running mates were wide and wild, half-filled with fear, half-filled with the thrill of some terrible adventure. Some unknown force pushed me to velocities which strained every muscle, as I ran amidst these strangely familiar faces. Higher reason escaped me, as if it had been overpowered by a demon in pursuit of some maddening scheme of revenge. We had challenged the offenders, the enemy, and hurried crazily to the appointed place of battle.

My mind was hazy and dim. I was unaware of anything other than the primary goal of this hostile pack of running youth. I vaguely remembered some happier existence, but where and when I could not recall. All I knew in that moment was that I was a member of the pack, that I belonged, and I liked the feeling of power that came from this belonging.

By ourselves alone, each of us felt unimportant, vulnerable, and insignificant. As a group, we were strong and instilled fear in others, gaining their fearful respect through strategies of tyranny and intimidation. As individuals we were simply the throwaways of society. We were the poor, the uneducated, the homeless, the hungry, the jobless. We were the Blacks, Chicanos, Asians, Puerto Ricans and White trash. We were the criminals, the mentally unbalanced, the juvenile delinquents, the hopeless. We were the rebels, the dangerous, the incorrigibles.

Society shunned us and we had little chance even to survive, much less to achieve success in a world that looked down upon us as little more than rubbish. We were usually ignored until we caused enough noise and destruction to gain attention to our needs. Why should we improve our behaviors when society had already judged and labeled us as scum, parasites, worthless, stupid and dirty? How could we ever change our ways when people of higher class and education turn their backs on us and wished that we did not exist? What ideals of respect and honor would we ever gain while being shut out from the rest of the world? What would we learn of love, compassion and integrity? We had heard of these things, yet when would someone dare to come into our realm and set an example for us so that we might learn how to change our behaviors?

We have only understood how to use force and abuse to get what we needed and wanted. We have understood that withholding of kindness bends others to our will. We have known no other way. We have had the experience of power only when we joined together and took our own action of revenge and retaliation on those who wronged us. And we have had to kill, steal, and terrorize in order to survive and remain in power. We have known no other way to feel a sense of self-worth.

We have known no other way to stop the hurt and emptiness we have felt inside because our lives and the outcome of our existence have already been pre-determined by the beliefs, judgments, and assumptions of an uncaring world. If we continue to be judged as the ne'er-do-wells of the world, would we ever do well? As long as we continue to be looked upon as the rats, parasites, and worms of the world, we would act like them. As long as we continue to be considered beyond help, we would remain so.

We grew up in families that were hostile or simply didn't care enough about us. The anger and resentment within us has been passed from generation to generation.

Few escaped our realm of the poor and unfortunate. Only those who were unusually strong and clear in their minds were able to grow beyond the boundaries of these limitations. And even then, they were lucky to have had a parent, a caretaker, a guardian, or teacher who encouraged them with hopeful words and enough loving support. What about the rest of us who never had that? Who would reach out to show us how to move beyond our limitations?

The upper class has thought of us as useless and a danger to them. We have been like the annoying and stubborn stains on their precious white satin gowns and silk dress shirts. But society does not know about the shame of unacceptance, the fear of being unwanted that motivates us into hateful and angry actions.

We have built evil empires and generated our own laws out of fear that we would not survive. When would society admit that we have been a part of the same world all along and that kindness, concern, compassion, and appropriate good will toward our kind would set the example for what we need to know?

Until that time comes, we continue to wander without direction, squandering our creative abilities on survival. We maintain a frightening world of power through intimidation in violent, dark kingdoms generated to enforce the illusion of safety and fleeting self-worth. Our children and our children's children will do the same, for all they could learn is through the example we have set.

Our violent and often ambivalent attitude seems justified, as society's opinions, judgments and perspectives keep us locked into miserable conditions.

We cheat, lie, steal, hurt, and kill in order that we might simply exist. We abuse drugs, chemicals, and alcohol to squelch the pain of emptiness we feel inside and to murder the voices in our heads that remind us over and over again of our low self-image and valuelessness.

As these unfamiliar thoughts swarmed painfully through my mind, and as my body contracted anxiously with feelings of worthlessness and hopelessness, I felt even more determined to prove my worth. Through the acknowledgment and acceptance received from this gang of wild-eyed youths, I achieved purpose and recognition.

These troubled thoughts vanished as we finally collided with our enemies in an old vacant parking lot. We clashed violently, thrashing and brandishing the full fervor of years of pent-up rage, fear, frustration, hatred and lack of worth with clubs, knives, machetes and guns. We fought only to win, to survive and to absorb the power of those who would give up or die. And we knew our enemies wanted the same from us.

The flashing of clenched teeth, the groans and grunts of scrapping, stabbing and punching abruptly ceased when something struck me hard on the head. In the same instant I hit the ground, the sound of gunshots rang out. Approaching sirens screamed in unison . . . and then there was silent blackness.

Groggy, I awoke on a cold, concrete floor. The lights were bright, and I squinted at the walls of putrid pale green all around me. Some of the others were here, lying on bare mattresses or sitting with backs against the walls. We were in a large jail cell, and the stench of body odor and urine was offensive. I looked around at my comrades. Everyone had some wound that had been barely treated and sparsely bandaged, probably by indifferent medical personnel.

There were bandages on my hand from cuts I did not know I had incurred in the bloody battle. The pain in my head reminded me of the blow which had rendered me unconscious. I should have been taken to the hospital; but no, that privilege was reserved for those who could afford the hospital fees or had insurance to cover expenses. I was one of the expendable ones, as were those who shared this jail cell with me.

As I studied the others, I observed the look of despair and aching sadness etched deeply on their faces. In their eyes was the longing for something . . . something we had not experienced but had heard about, read about, and seen in movies: nurturing, understanding, acceptance, respect, opportunity. We wanted those things, especially now as we wallowed in the heavy air of an uncertain future. We did not know how to create those things in our lives because we had never had them.

I felt the abandonment we all knew — abandonment by our parents, caretakers, teachers and authority figures who could not or would not give us the love, support and encouragement we needed to help us develop into healthy, balanced individuals; abandonment by a society that did not acknowledge our existence except to generate charitable organizations and programs that simply placed a small band-aid on an enormous, gaping wound.

As I observed all of them in this sad jail room, my head throbbed violently. Dizzy and nauseated, I slumped to the floor. The pain was excruciating, unbearable; then it suddenly stopped. I felt myself lifting gently off the floor, and floating effortlessly upward toward the ceiling. Looking down, I saw my dead body curled into a ball. Several comrades were gathered around, shaking the lifeless form, crying and shouting. Relieved to be done with it, I did not care about my body any more, but my heart went out to those left behind, those lost and lonely souls of the world.

The ache in my chest was not from mortal wounds. It was a deep longing for these incorrigibles to be set free from the bondage they endured. I prayed that they might find a way to let love into their hearts and to keep society from dictating how they should think about themselves. I visualized them finding hope and strength to achieve their dreams and the right to live happy and fulfilling lives.

Sighing deeply, I drew my attention away from them. I noticed a bright light, and as I turned slowly toward it I saw Divine Mother standing next to me. Upon recognizing her, all memory of my identity came flooding back. I was Clarion once more.

"Oh, my God! I can't believe what just happened," I exclaimed, as tears welled in my eyes. "I was in that body.

I was someone else and forgot all about myself and everything I had ever known. It was wild. I had this entire experience of being . . . "

Choking on my words, I sobbed, partly from relief at being freed from that unhappy, hopeless life, and partly from sorrow for those I left behind in that cell filled with sullen faces. Divine Mother responded.

"All of the troubled ones of your world suffer the same despair and lack of love," she announced softly, with compassionate concern in her voice that seemed weighted with the passing of millenniums. "As you have pursued this journey with me, you have desired many times, Clarion, to be back in the beautiful meadow. You wanted only to feel good. You did not want to see, or accept, the shadow side of human nature.

"You are like most people in your world who act as though the shadow side of human nature and the darker side of society is evil. You, and others like yourself, do not want to look at or acknowledge anything that is unpleasant or uncomfortable.

"Those of you who consider yourselves enlightened very often overlook the ever-present fact that you are all connected and related to one another. Everyone on your planet is your brother and sister, regardless of how they behave. You can easily accept this idea of brotherly and sisterly love and unity as long as everything goes nicely and everyone is well behaved. Yet the moment that others act in ways that bring discomfort or unpleasantness, you reject them and judge them as the bad ones, the enemy and the cause of evil in life. Little do you realize that you reject portions of yourself in the process; you reject the uncomfortable and unpleasant aspects that exist within you, but that you do not want to accept.

"You use enormous amounts of energy to create a mask, a false self-image, that you hope will hide the unpleasant traits within you from others. This is the shadow nature. As long as it is rejected, denied, and feared, the shadow nature within humanity and within each person will remain in control. It will deplete your creative life energies and will act itself out in unconscious, self-defeating, and destructive ways."

She was right. I had covered up my real feelings and intentions in many situations and had pretended to have my act together just to keep things pleasant. Over time I had become more honest, more authentic with myself and others. I now know that I still have work to do in the areas of greater self-acceptance and in accepting others, no matter what part in life they play. Also I know that being more accepting and understanding of my shadow nature will bring a new freedom for me that I truly welcome.

A bright, soft mist gradually enveloped us, and Divine Mother coaxed me to lie down and rest. The despair of my last experience still reverberated within me. An ocean of light washed over and through me, lifting away the remaining sadness and pain. I breathed fully again and it felt good. Relaxing into peace, I listened to Divine Mother as she spoke again.

"Everyone deserves to be in the beautiful meadow, Clarion. The 'beautiful meadow' is a symbol for the God presence and the fertile, lush soil of the Creative Life Force inside of each person. It is a symbol of peace, beauty, wholeness, clarity, wisdom and truth, which each person can claim. If they do not know that the meadow exists, or if they do not know how to get there, how will they ever experience peace of mind, love and beauty within themselves? It will take someone who knows the way to guide them in the right direction, and bring them into the light of understanding."

My mind turned over and over the words that she spoke, as I thought about the more unfortunate ones of the world. Our societies have many inappropriate judgments about those we believe to be inferior to us. I have turned my nose up at hostile youths and welfare recipients. I have been repulsed by sick and disabled people. I did not want to deal with them beyond the comfort of the Presidential office. It was easier to interact with all of these unpleasant situations through the organizations that tried to help them. I did not have to get close to any of it. I realized that it was my fearful judgments that kept me from fully understanding and accepting these people. It was guilt that motivated my support of charitable organizations whose programs did not even begin to address the root cause of the problems.

I believed that by donating money, granting federal assistance and passing certain legislation for community improvement programs, I was doing my good deed. I even believed that I would be considered a good person and a great humanitarian. I laughed at myself, for this was only my way to quell the embarrassment and guilt for the judgments I held, and my inability to embrace reality.

Divine Mother went on: "When you have judgments upon another person and have identified him as being incurable, bad or evil, worthless or no good, stupid or incompetent, you have placed a limitation upon that person to a greater or lesser degree.

"When hundreds, thousands, even millions of people share the same critical judgments about a particular individual or group of people, then the possibilities for transforming their condition are thwarted. It is much more difficult to improve an unpleasant condition when critical thoughts, misinformation, and shallow judgments prevail, whether in the family or in the world at large. Someone who commits atrocities, for example, will have great difficulty in realizing how to change his behavior; in fact, his condition is only amplified by the critical and hateful judgments he feels from others."

Remembering myself as the young man running through the alleys, blending with his thoughts and feelings as if they were my own, I recalled his longing for acceptance and the opportunities that other members of society merely took for granted. He had human needs and yearnings like everyone else. The circumstances he was born into created an almost insurmountable obstacle, a difficult challenge that most others in society did not have to face. This was true of the disabled, Third World populations and the uneducated. It was true, as well, with regard to racial differences and gender issues. How can we change this?

Divine Mother touched me on the shoulder, gestured for me to rise, and pointed silently into the bright mist that enveloped us. Sitting up, I peered into a clearing in the wispy radiance, and saw a limpid pool of crystalline liquid before me.

As the liquid thickened and expanded, I saw a vision within the mysterious substance. I watched intently as the more unfortunate people of the world received loving and concerned attention from caring individuals, communities and nations. They were provided with free education in the realm of self-appreciation, self-esteem and self-love. They learned about, and came to accept, their unique value and place in the world. They were treated as equals, brothers and sisters who were perhaps less fortunate in some ways, but recognized for their value as human beings.

Through this kind of education they discovered the importance of beauty, harmony, health, respect, honor, honesty, integrity, and social contribution. They saw how these values improved their lives and rippled out into the lives of others. It was difficult for some to learn and to apply these concepts, since they had experienced so many years of social inferiority and hardship. However, extra diligence and patience with these individulas yielded powerful results.

As I stared into this "looking-glass," I witnessed the effects of this education in their children and their children's children. Parents were provided with special education in the areas of healthy child-rearing, and their children were happier and better adjusted. They developed personal security and healthier life styles. Both parents' and children's education included courses in personal self-worth and spirituality, with emphasis placed upon individual and social responsibility.

Children learned at a very young age how important they were, that their very existence influenced and interrelated with every other person and every other living thing. They grew up with a healthy respect for themselves, each other, and all of nature. They were taught about the power of a calm mind and loving behavior. The happy faces, laughing children, and healthy living brought tears of yearning to my eyes.

Because of the differences this made in the children, the cities began to take on a new look, a new atmosphere. Slums were cleaned up and renovated. Grass, flowers and trees were planted in vacant lots. Old, useless buildings were torn down and replaced with community gardens and playgrounds for the children. Community endeavors expanded to include the elderly. It was found that their many years of experience helped to resolve important community challenges, while their value as nurturing caretakers of the children and the neighborhood gardens proved to be of priceless worth.

The homeless, the jobless, the disabled, and the handicapped found creative outlets that contributed to the world in ways that delighted them and served others. The hungry were fed. The sick were healed. The number of incorrigibles dwindled as self-appreciation and individual and social responsibility replaced the need to violate or abuse others. They had discovered that healthy and balanced life-styles were far more rewarding and fulfilling.

I felt a pang in my heart as I looked upon these visions. It was the beginning of heaven on earth.

"Is this possible?" I turned to Divine Mother, doubtful that what she was showing me could be created in our world. "I would be overjoyed, ecstatic, happy beyond description if humanity could live this way. Why have you shown me these things? What can I do about it?"

Her whimsical smile seemed to imply that I should know the answer.

TEN

The bright mist dissolved, and I found myself sitting cross-legged on the wild grasses of the beautiful meadow. The sun shone in brilliant fashion and warmed my chilled body. As I glanced around, I saw vivid colors everywhere and appreciated more than ever the beauty of this place. The sharpness of detail was astounding and brought me back abruptly into present reality. The contrast caused my experience to seem more like a dream, and I wondered if it all really happened.

I was content to be still and quiet with my thoughts, when from behind me two small arms suddenly embraced my neck and a little body pressed itself against mine. "It's about time you woke up."

"Mathias, you're here!" Reaching around, I pulled him into my lap and held him close. I had not realized until now how much I missed him; and whether because of my awesome journey or some other reason, I felt so much more grateful for him and for life itself.

"What do you mean, it's about time I woke up? I've been very busy. I've had enough experiences to last a lifetime . . . many lifetimes." Grinning so widely that I thought my face might crack, I chuckled with amazement at what I had gone through.

"You were sleeping here in the meadow for just a little while." Mathias was wide-eyed as he spoke, clutching my sweater with his small hands. "Divine Mother said that you were on an important journey. She said that your body was here, but that you were somewhere else. I know what that means because it's happened to me. It's not dreaming, you know. It's actually happening. Wherever you went, and whatever you did, it really happened!"

"It certainly seemed real. I saw so much and learned so much." I looked down at the ground and thought again of the events I had just witnessed. "I don't think I will ever be the same after this."

"Well, you're not done yet. There's more to come!" With a cocky smirk, Mathias leaped off my lap. He hopped onto a large boulder, stood regally upon it, and held a long stick as if he were a king of some imaginary kingdom.

"What do you mean, I'm not done yet? I feel very well done as a matter of fact. I don't need to have more lessons! I'm overloaded as it is with what I've learned." I searched the meadow for Divine Mother, but she was nowhere to be seen. "I've been here too long. It's time for me to go home."

"Thou shalt not whine!" Mathias commanded, waving the long stick in my direction as though it were a royal scepter. "Come hither and I shall dub thee a knight of the Holy Order, and thou shalt have renewed strength to continue on thy journey."

"Mathias, this is no time to clown around. Haven't we had enough? I mean . . . haven't *I* had enough? You only play and have a good time while I'm going through some very traumatic situations." I folded my arms across my chest, incensed at his oblivious attitude.

"Lighten up. You're much too serious. You turn everything into a major ordeal. Haven't you learned yet to live in the moment and appreciate your experiences? Aren't you grateful for what Divine Mother has shown you?" He sat down in a huff, disappointed with my lack of playfulness.

"I'm a grown-up, Mathias, " I bellowed, then immediately felt a little foolish at becoming so upset with him. "I have responsibilities. I'm the President of the United States. I need to get back home and resume my job. People are counting on me. You're only a kid. You don't understand."

Mathias shook his head slowly, as if I was a difficult student. Maybe I *was* a difficult student. Nevertheless, the responsibilities of my role in life were calling me. It seemed that many days had passed, and that made me all the more anxious to return home.

"What day is this, Mathias?"

He smiled mischieviously, ignoring my question as he jumped off the rock and ran toward the temple.

Beckoning with a wave of his arm, he turned and yelled, "Follow me!", then skipped up the steps and stood in the center of the platform.

"What's going to happen this time?" I groaned.

"Come on, Clarion!" Mathias shouted, still waving for me to follow. "You're the one who's so concerned with time, so you'd better hurry up. The 'cosmic train' is leaving!"

A mysterious power took hold of my feet and it seemed as if they moved all by themselves. I resisted in my mind, but my body kept moving forward toward the temple. Insatiable curiosity arose within me, even as my mind was screaming in total rebellion.

As I approached the platform, Mathias held out his hand. Hesitating, I glanced around the meadow once more for any signs of Divine Mother. I thought perhaps I would see her again if I followed Mathias. After my harrowing experiences, however, I was afraid to risk it.

I remembered my heart center, the Heart-Mind, as Divine Mother had called it. Centering myself once again into that special place, the thoughts of fear faded, and enthusiasm filled me. I did not know what dangers awaited this time, but the promise of another adventure and important lessons to be learned suddenly took on greater importance. Feeling as though I must be mad, I allowed my heart to win out over my head. I reached out and took his hand.

Standing beside him, I drew in a long, deep breath and let it out completely. The familiar tingling of energy fizzed and buzzed all around me. Sparkling gold and white light grew brighter and brighter, and I watched as the smiling face of Mathias disappeared completely.

The familiar spinning sensation returned. I resisted it at first, but then remembered to relax and to keep breathing deeply. The brightness receded and I found myself flying low over the earth. I did not know where I was, but rising up quickly beneath me was the brilliant turquoise blue of a great ocean, and I was fast approaching a large island. The scene was extraordinary, and I was awestruck.

Sailing now over the shores of the land, a great city spread far and wide before me. I studied the panorama of hundreds of thousands of sun-bleached dwellings, crowded tightly together and spilling profusely over small hills and shallow valleys. Near the center of this huge metropolis were several massive structures, supported by huge columns of white marble.

The view conjured up memories of Athens, Greece. I had traveled there many years ago and was greatly impressed with the ancient ruins and the evidence of their masterful architecture. The atmosphere of the city had such a peaceful and happy influence upon me, that when it was time to return to the States, I had a deep regret. Yet if what I am seeing now is truly Athens, Greece, it is no longer in ruin.

Approaching what appeared to be the Parthenon, I

could easily see hundreds of people in the unpaved streets. The simple tunic-style clothing, the donkeys, horses, carts, and non-existence of modern vehicles or facilities suggested that I may have traveled back in time.

And where was Mathias? Realizing I was alone, I felt a strong and sudden pull toward the crowds in the street, and was drawn sharply toward one man who strolled briskly along a dusty thoroughfare.

The next thing I knew, I was walking in sandals and noticed the dust covering my toes and leather straps. The day was warm, and a balmy sea breeze caressed my face and rippled quietly through the loose garment that covered my perspiring body.

I had been walking since mid-morning through the crowded marketplace and felt compelled by some anticipation, some exciting rendezvous. I was happy and appreciative of the day.

In the leather bag which hung from my shoulders was a precious gift for someone special. I smiled as I imagined the delight of my lover upon receiving the surprise gift.

Lover? Do I have a lover? Feeling suddenly disoriented, I stopped short in the midst of the bustling crowd. I was seeing flashes of another existence, in which I was a much older and very important person in a powerful land. Surely it's just a daydream, a fantasy. For a moment I did not know where I was. I felt as though I was someone else in some other place. Oh well, there was nothing to be worried about. It was a great day and I resumed my journey, feeling glad to be alive.

Leaving the noise and hustle of the main street, I turned up a familiar narrow walkway that led to one of my favorite places in the city. The people of this neighbor-hood took great pride in planting and tending beautiful gardens which spilled out onto the public walkways.

Friendliness abounded, and as I waved to people in windows or to others who were gathering flowers and herbs in their yards, they smiled and waved back to me.

An extravagant fountain adorned the center court of this neighborhood. The architecture of the fountain flourished with carvings of cherubs, dolphins and other creatures, generating a wild panoply of playful vitality. Water from an ancient artesian well gushed abundantly from deep caverns within Mother Earth, and the fountain artfully channeled this water into a large pool, where men and women dipped their clay jars and small children splashed one another. I paused for a moment to survey the pleasant scene, and then resumed my journey up the gradual stone incline.

My gaze raced far ahead to a quaint dwelling nestled tightly among the others; and I saw Adoni, my lover, bounding out of the door. I waved excitedly, my heart leaping with joy.

As Adoni waited for me at the edge of a lavishly landscaped garden, I admired the shape of my lover's body, its attractive contours slightly revealed under the loose sheath of a flowing white tunic. It draped casually over poised shoulders and ended at the knees, exposing youthful, trim legs. A wide band of bronze and silver gathered the cloth to a soft cinch around the slender waist, and a small wood carving of a dolphin quivered at the end of a braided chain, which hung around the waist as well.

Adoni reached out with open arms, drawing me into a warm embrace, and I kissed him passionately on the lips. I jerked away from him, and looked upon the face of the man I loved. For a fleeting moment, I felt a vague repulsion, as though this was wrong. He was a man and so was I. And yet the powerful attraction that I felt for him was undeniable.

"What's the matter? Is something wrong?"

Adoni queried, as his eyebrows knit tightly into a curious peak above his nose. He gently touched my cheek as his large pale blue eyes searched the depth of my being. Those eyes reminded me of someone else, someone I knew and cared about, but whom I could not remember.

"No, no, nothing is wrong. It was just a strange feeling. I . . . I . . . c-can't explain it," I stammered, "except that for a moment it was as though I was someone else who had a life in some other place. The same thing happened earlier this morning while I was walking here. Just now, I had the feeling that what we were doing was wrong, that it was unacceptable for two men to be lovers." I spoke these words apprehensively, not wanting to offend or hurt Adoni in any way.

"What? Oh, how silly. I've never heard of such a thing. We've been lovers for years. Why would you suddenly feel this way?" He took my hand, not waiting for an answer, and led me into his home.

I loved coming to Adoni's home. He was a master at creating a warm and inviting environment. He displayed his love and knowledge of fine art, flowers, plants, and furnishings with a vibrant flair, and I never ceased to admire and appreciate his talent. Making sure that I was comfortable, he went into the other room, and I could hear the familiar clinking of earthen jars and bowls. He returned, smiling, and handed me my favorite silver cup. It was filled to the brim with a cherished burgundy wine, imported from the rich lands to the north and across the sea. Adoni sat down next to me, touching the rim of his cup to mine, and we sipped the wine in silence.

I sighed heavily, confused with my earlier response to Adoni. How could I question my feelings for him after all this time? I was so fortunate to have found such a loving and caring soul. I felt as if I had been overly blessed by his devotion. His presence added so much good to my life.

I particularly enjoyed our long, deep-into-the-night conversations about various spiritual philosophies. We spoke often of Sophocles, Aristotle, and Socrates. We also enjoyed the challenge of the bow and arrow, and as a team won many awards and honors in the public archery competitions.

We both loved the Oracle at Mount Andira and would make the long trek to her mountain sanctuary just to hear her speak for an afternoon. Hundreds of respectful citizens would do the same on appointed sacred days. We would all sit or recline on the hillside, sharing baskets of food while waiting patiently for her appearance. The atmosphere was always one of high enthusiasm, both from the crowd's anticipation and from the elevation of consciousness that everyone experienced simply by being in the presence of the Oracle.

"Adoni," I slowly began, "remember the time when we went to the Oracle and she said something greatly disturbing about the future?"

"She has said many greatly disturbing things about the future, many of which have already come to pass. Which disturbing things are you referring to?" Adoni cocked his head and teasingly raised an eyebrow.

"The one about the New Atlantis, the new land to the west that would become the most prosperous and powerful nation on earth. She said that the people of that land would distort many spiritual truths and they would be swayed into worshipping a god that judged people as being either good or bad. She said that the people of that mighty land would use the power of a corrupt government and religious dogma to do away with certain types of people and behavior that were offensive to the self-righteous." I paused, unsure if I wanted to continue.

"Yes, yes, go on. What are you trying to say?" Adoni fidgeted nervously as he waited for me to continue.

116

"She said that the New Atlantis will express both the light and the dark personas in extreme polarities, and that the darkness in individuals and societies will be projected out onto those who will be judged as living in sin." Hesitating again, I took a deep breath and went on. "She said that in that nation, the people will consider it unacceptable and sinful for members of the same sex to be lovers. The people in that land will do terrible things to them, forcing them go into hiding or to be secretive about their lifestyles.

"She said that before that great nation is birthed, there will be a frightening period of darkness in old Europe. Women who honor the Goddess and men who have male lovers will be put to death in a most horrid fashion." A feeling of great sadness washed through me as I imagined the possibility of such a dismal future.

"Are you becoming upset over something that's not supposed to happen for another thousand years or more?" Adoni jumped up, spilling wine from his cup, and paced up and down the floor with one hand on his hip. "I can't believe you're getting so upset about this. Lighten up! You're much too serious. You turn everything into a major ordeal. Haven't you learned yet to live in the moment?"

Where had I heard him say that before? Startled, it seemed as though I was experiencing something from another lifetime, an event which was accepted as commonplace among the Greeks.

"You worry too often without any good reason. Can't you just be appreciative of the present and the fact that we're together? No one in this country would ever persecute us for being lovers. What we do and how we live is a natural thing! Can't you be happy about that?" Adoni didn't get upset often, but when he did, his face flushed a golden red, making him even more attractive.

"Come here." I held out my hand to him. "Come. I

almost forgot about the gift I brought for you."

He pouted defiantly, but then broke into a grin.
"All right, I give in. I'll not be upset anymore." He sat
down next to me, shoving me playfully with his shoulder.
"What did you bring me?"

Reaching into my leather bag, I pulled out a small,
carved, ivory box and placed it in his hands.

"Ahhh! It's exquisite! It's beautiful! Wherever did
you get this?" he exclaimed, cupping the box in his hands
as if it were a rare and expensive find.

"The real gift is inside. Go ahead . . . open it." I was
delighted with his pleasure.

Upon opening the box, his eyes and mouth fell open
like a surprised child. I loved his enthusiasm for the gifts
I gave to him. It was so easy to please Adoni.

"It's the most beautiful dolphin I have ever seen," he
gasped as he held the clear, crystal dolphin up to the light
of the window. He rotated it gleefully to catch a glimpse of
the tiny rainbow that shimmered inside the dolphin pre-
cisely at the spot where its heart would be.

"Whatever did I do to deserve such a wonderful
gift?" He knelt down at my feet and hugged my legs,
pressing his cheek against my knees.

"No special reason – just for being you. You have
given so much to me, Adoni. I cannot put a price on what
I have learned from you and the endless love and support
you have given to me over the years." Reaching down, I
ran my finger through his blonde, curly hair, wondering
again about the words of the Oracle. It was hard for me to
imagine a society where same-sex lovers were judged as
immoral or evil. It seemed to be a rather barbaric attitude
for an advanced civilization.

The Oracle had also said that amazing technology,
preoccupation with things of the mind, and worship of a
fearful and wrathful god of judgment would be honored

more than love, good will, and kindness toward each other.

I shivered when I thought of the dark era that would swallow Europe, hurting and killing people because of their differences in lifestyle and beliefs.

Adoni and I have never harmed anyone. We only want to live our lives in peace and to enjoy each other's company. We don't expect others to live our way if that's not their choice. Our families and our many loving friends have never treated us any differently than they have treated anyone else whom they love and care about. They have never been ashamed of us in any way. In fact, I have never known anyone in our culture who could not accept same sex lovers. Therefore, it was difficult for me to understand how any culture could consider a lifestyle such as ours as abnormal or threatening in any way.

I recalled the time long ago, before I met Adoni, when I liked a young woman. I saw her often and admired her deeply. We were great friends, and I thought that perhaps she would become my life mate. We began to make plans for a ceremony and feast to celebrate our desire to be together.

When I met Adoni, however, there was something so magnetic, so powerful between us. I did not understand the attraction at first, and I was torn between my lovely woman friend and Adoni for many months, until I could no longer deny my feelings: I had to be with Adoni. She was sad and hurt for a while and resentful of Adoni; but now she is happily joined to a young man who pleases her far more than I ever could. She has completely accepted Adoni and me with love and friendship.

Adoni looked up to me and asked, "What are you thinking about? You seem so far away."

"I was just thinking about the past, of things that happened a long time ago." I sighed, touching him lightly on the cheek.

"You're thinking about *her* again, aren't you?" he

queried, as an old familiar jealousy flashed in his eyes.

Amused, I responded teasingly, "After all this time you still worry that I might have regrets about my choice to be with you instead of her? Can't you be appreciative of the present and the fact that we're together?" Adoni laughed at the irony of my comment and pushed me roughly. We tumbled into a wrestling match, and pitted our greatest physical strength against each other. We often settled our disagreements and frustrations in this way, ending the strenuous bouts exhausted, at peace and content with one another once more.

Finally at rest in a sweaty heap upon the floor, we held each other, too tired to continue. We soon fell asleep, awakening in the early evening to prepare a light meal before daylight was lost. Afterwards, feeling delighted and satisfied, I joined Adoni in his bed and remained there for the night.

I was jolted from a sound sleep in the darkness of the night to loud banging on the door, and boisterous shouting and yelling of many voices. Gasping, I grabbed Adoni by the shoulder and shook hard.

"Adoni! Adoni! Wake up, wake up! Something is going on. There are people at the door." Hopping to our feet and fumbling with our clothing, we ran to the door half-naked.

When the door was unbolted, we were greeted by a mob of angry people. They lunged forward with blazing torches that cast bright flickering lights on raging faces and strange attire. A short, paunchy man stepped forward and held up his hand to quiet the crowd. He drew out a large roll of paper, unraveled it, and began to read out loud.

"Both of you have been charged with actions which are indecent, sinful, and evil in the eyes of the Lord and the good and just people of this land," he bellowed, as the crowd responded in agreement.

As he went on reading from the document, I whispered, "Adoni, do you understand what's going on here?" I turned to him to see his face illuminated by the flames and was shocked to see, not Adoni, but someone else — yet with the same familiar pale blue eyes. Wide-eyed and astonished, I stood there speechless.

"We've been found out, that's what it's all about. And why do you keep calling me Adoni? You must have been having one of those dreams again. All I know is that this is no dream. This is real, and we're in big trouble." His voice trembled and light reflected on the tears that glistened in his eyes.

He looked longingly at me as the love of years and the kaleidoscope of many lifetimes flashed across his face: he was Adoni, next he was a beautiful woman, then another man, once more my lover, after that a young maiden and finally a young boy named Mathias.

Mathias, the little boy in the meadow! I felt the blood drain from my face as vague memories invaded my awareness. Who was I? Where was I? I glanced down at my body and saw clothing of a dark, coarse weave suggestive of another era.

I stared in disbelief into the face of my lover. My confusion was tormenting, and I scarcely heard the drone of the paunchy man's voice as it faded into the background, finally coming to an abrupt end. My reverie was broken when the mob of hostile men and women clamored toward the door, and yanked both of us out into the street.

Our wrists were tied tightly behind our backs with thick, prickly rope, and we were poked, swatted and batted

121

with long, heavy sticks. In this atrocious fashion, they forced us towards the commoners' square in the center of town.

The crowd rallied like a starved-crazed pack of wolves, their faces mimicking those of jackals and ghouls, sardonically grinning in anticipation of the event to come. The terror was excruciating as I lost sight of my lover – or was he Mathias? I was so confused I could not think as repeated blows to my head, shoulders, and buttocks quelled all reasoning. Blood trickled into my eyes and mingled with the tears that streamed down my face. I felt sudden rage, growled and gnashed my teeth like a wild animal, only to be kicked and beaten some more until my will was broken. I would do anything now to stop the hurting. My pleas for mercy went unheard, among the deafening din of the mad hysteria.

When the gruesome parade came to a halt in the square, the horrible cacophony ceased and voices were hushed. The paunchy man with the unraveled paper began to speak once more. Wearily raising my head, I looked at him as he stood arrogantly in front of a huge pile of wood, in the center of which a tall pole had been erected. I watched in horror as a woman I knew was bound by chains to the pole. Nausea welled up from the pit of my stomach.

As the man went on with his theatrical blaring, the proclamation of the woman's diabolic witchery fell upon the ears of the hundreds of townspeople. They both feared and hated the discovered witches, women who days earlier had been their neighbors and friends. Somehow, I had memories of this woman and knew her to be a compassionate healer, a true servant of the common folk, and an honorable practitioner of the sacred ways of the Great Goddess, the Divine Mother.

My companion and I had great respect and love for

her, often bringing her rare and prized herbs from difficult mountain trails and faraway valleys. She had healed the sick and helped so many to lead healthier lives. Sadly, her way of life and service eventually caused her to be charged with unequivocal heresy. And because my companion and I were found out to be lovers, we were named as her evil consorts, in league with the devil himself! The shock of this pronouncement stunned me, and the sound of someone retching and choking drew my attention to the bent-over form of my companion, my lover, my friend. Helpless to comfort him, I wept profusely, no longer caring whether I lived or died.

Someone shouted hoarsely that there were not enough kindling sticks to start the fire, "There is not enough faggot wood here, sir. We need faggots!" A few eager bystanders began the anxious search for proper kindling to ignite the blaze.

"Wait! Look at these two," cried another as he pointed his bony finger at my companion and me. "Their clothing and hair will be enough to start the fire burning. Let us use *them* as the faggot wood to kindle the flames."

A gleeful roar exploded from the multitude, and I felt I was about to faint. It would be most merciful now if I could slip into unconsciousness. In desperation, I began to pray to the Mother Goddess.

My companion and I were dragged on our knees to the pile of wood, and our legs were wrapped together like faggot wood with bailing twine.

I cast a last gaze upon my friend while he struggled to look at me with the remainder of his strength. When our eyes met, I knew without a doubt who he was. I sent him my deepest feelings of love and gratitude.

We both were overwhelmed with tears, and the face of my companion blurred into the surroundings. Then, we were tossed cruelly onto the pile of wood. One torch was held close to my clothing and another at the hair of my head.

Suddenly I felt an indescribable searing pain that cracked and whipped its way across my face and down my back, engulfing my feet. I became aware of the screaming and shrieking that rose from my own throat. After that, I knew nothing more of bodily sensation, as I floated like fine mist above the blazing scene. I beheld the blackened bodies consumed in flames, thrashing about like the legs of dead frogs that jerk and jump hideously when immersed in boiling water.

My only concern was for the safety of the souls of my companion and the woman. It was a dreadful sight. My concern finally gave way to detachment, as I floated higher and began to tumble gently in a soft white light. Its presence enfolded me completely, bringing peace and serenity. The sensations of pain and confusion ebbed away, and at last, although a little weary, I began to feel whole and content again. The buzz of the soothing presence pulsed rhythmically, like tranquil ocean waves lapping gently upon a sandy shore.

The refreshing rhythm subsided, leaving me to rest on something solid. I blinked a few times in the brilliant sunlight and squinted to observe blurry treetops against the vivid blue sky. Turning my head to one side, I was surprised to see Mathias lying next to me, staring at me with those familiar large, pale blue eyes.

I yelled, and I sat up quickly. "Mathias! What happened? I thought I was in another lifetime, two lifetimes. And you were there . . . I think . . . and . . . and . . ." I found myself unable to speak of the disturbing events.

"Wasn't it awesome?" Mathias chirped with delight, as though he had just returned from a casual afternoon at the movies. "You were great."

"What do you mean, 'It was awesome' and 'I was

great"? It was horrible! Terrible! I'll never use that word 'faggot' again, not ever! I had no idea that's where that term came from." Holding my hands over my eyes, I could not believe he was so apathetic.

"I am not ap . . . apath . . . whatever that word is that you were thinking about. I do care. I simply have a different way of looking at those things, that's all." Sitting up, he beamed at me and seemed wiser than ever before. My past life experiences with him were difficult to accept. However, it could explain why I was so fond of him and had so easily trusted him from the beginning.

"How can you not see the tragedy of that last life? You and I both went through incredible pain and torture. Those people were barbaric! It must have been during the Inquisition period in Old Europe. It's awful what they did. I'll never forget it, ever!" I clenched my fists and clamped my jaw. I wanted to get even with those who murdered us.

"The need to get even . . . that is precisely how hate and hostility prevail in your world." Divine Mother's voice was clear as she appeared out of nowhere.

I was so pleased to see her that I ignored her statement and began blurting out the story of my experience. She held up her hand to stop me.

"Yes, Clarion, I observed it all. I know what happened." She gently pried, "What did you learn from those lives?"

"Well, if you saw it all, then you saw those people behaving as wild, vicious animals! What they did was inexcusable! Horrible! That's what I learned. I'm tired of going through these experiences. I'm worn out, confused, and darn near delirious." With great drama I emphasized my emotional state to add impact and to elicit some sympathy from Divine Mother. "I've died twice now! My body can't take any more brutality. "

125

"The soul is eternal."

"That may be so," I barked back, "but my body isn't eternal." Jumping to my feet, I stomped back and forth across the grass. "My body felt the pain and all the emotions. It experienced all the feelings!"

"Clarion," she softly coaxed, "What did you learn?"

Grumbling, I kicked a few stones around, sat on a small boulder and stared at the tops of the trees at the far end of the meadow. Breathing deeply and pulling my attention into my heart center, I began to feel clearer and less angry. My thoughts began to come into focus.

"All right, all right. It's true that I have had judgments about homosexuals, cruel judgments." It was embarrassing to admit it. "I have never harmed any of them, not directly anyway, but I have participated in some nasty joke telling at parties. I have never attempted to befriend homosexuals; in fact, I have intentionally avoided them. Its repulsive to see men kissing other men as lovers do." I hung my head, ashamed of myself as I recalled the life-time in Ancient Greece.

"I have a different perspective now. I'm willing to accept that a man can love another man deeply, passionately and romantically, no less deeply than one heterosexual can love another heterosexual. This must be true as well for a woman who loves another woman." Searching Divine Mother's face for acceptance, I went on, "It is true that in the past I have considered homosexuals to be second-class citizens."

"And . . ." she added emphatically, "You have purposely procrastinated in passing specific legislation in Congress designed to ensure that the rights of homosexuals would be protected."

I winced when she exposed that issue. My face flushed with guilt as I attempted to defend my actions with a less-than-convincing tone, "I'm pressured by many special interest groups and religious organizations. Even though there had been improvements in the areas of homosexual rights, there are many people in this country who have extreme judgments about their lifestyle. And who can blame them for their judgments when we see how homosexuals behave? They flaunt their differences in public places, offending even those who support gay issues!"

The energy field surrounding Divine Mother flashed like red lightning, and her eyes became intense and unyielding. Feeling that I may have offended her, I prepared to run for cover. In an instant, she became calmer and responded sternly to what I had just said.

"You focus on the more extreme examples of homosexuality, on the few who are rebellious and angry. Many of them bring into this present life subconscious memories of mass persecutions, torturous abuse and cruel executions in other lifetimes. They display their rage and resentment in a variety of ways, and of course, this gains a great deal of attention from the media. This has generated the belief that all homosexuals are this way, which is not true. Most homosexuals simply want to live quietly and peacefully and do not wish to offend anyone. They want to be left alone to their own choice of lifestyle and not to be persecuted because of it.

"Remember, Clarion, in the eyes of God, the Beloved Creator, all human beings are precious. All living things are sacred. Each person has been eternally endowed with the birthright of free will: the freedom to choose for themselves how they will express what is natural for *them*. The Beloved Creator does not judge people as being good or evil." Her intonation seemed scolding, and I felt the blush in my face.

"Many present-day homosexuals were persecutors of homosexuals in previous lives and are now living as homosexuals in order to balance the karmic scales. Your rejection of homosexuals is your way of getting even, since some of them were the very ones who persecuted you."

Divine Mother continued as my head sank lower and lower into my shoulders, like a turtle pulling into its shell. "By purposely withholding your attention from that legislation, you are robbing them of their right to be treated as equal human beings. Through your critical judgments and actions, you are treating them the way they treated you. And because your homosexual lifestyle ended in a painful death in that lifetime, you have chosen to reject homosexuality in this life as a way to protect yourself from ridicule, and to gurantee society's acceptance."

It was quite startling to realize that I had been battling with the same individuals again. It was just as startling to realize that I had become someone who was as abusive in some ways as those who had been cruel to me and judged me unfairly in past lives.

I thought this over, pondering the idea of judgments. Why do we judge others in the way that we do? What makes us want to persecute certain types of people? When we judge others, it seems to be out of fear and misunderstanding of their actions and behavior.

I shared my thoughts with Divine Mother. "Perhaps when we judge others, we are trying to gain control of the situation by making ourselves right. If we make someone else wrong for his behavior, we can feel that we are right and superior. We feel good about ourselves when we are right, and force the power and energy to come our way. Having power over others seems to be how we create security for ourselves. It's the same thing as monopolizing power, isn't it?"

"In a way," she partially agreed. "Realize, however, that the use of judgment in itself is not wrong. Judgment is necessary in your world in order to make sound and appropriate assessments of specific situations, to discern how you will interact with and respond to certain conditions and events in life. Trouble occurs when you use judgments to make someone else wrong so that you can be right, superior, and in control."

"Speaking of judgment," I responded, "What about our judicial system? We're required at times to judge members of our society through a jury system. What can you say about that?" Anxious to hear what she had to say, I positioned myself comfortably on the flat rock and waited, relieved that I had successfully diverted the conversation to a new topic.

I glanced at Mathias, who was playing among the flowers with little interest in such adult concerns. I envied that child-like lack of concern for a moment. The simplicity of a child's life seemed so attractive, so much more sensible at times.

Divine Mother's energy field pulsated with a vibrant golden-yellow as she spoke. "Your present judicial system originated from a very ancient system intended to restore planetary equilibrium when conditions had fallen out of balance. The original foundation for this ancient system, as it presently exists in your world, was spiritually conceived and was structured specifically for the cultures of earth. Even though your present system has been corrupted and misused by irresponsible and power hungry individuals, remnants of the original law remain in action in your modern day judicial system.

"When the sacred ways and the original law were abused and forgotten by humankind through the original separation and fall from Godhood, it was necessary to create a system that would re-establish and maintain balance in your world so that humankind would not annihilate itself. When humankind fell from Godhood, with each soul falling from unity with the Godhead or Higher Self, spiritual darkness fell upon the earth. This sleep of forgetfulness generated a deep denial and separation from wholeness which split into many parts or fragments within the individual self or soul. The human soul was no longer whole, no longer holy . . . no longer integrated or at peace with itself.

"In your present day judicial system, the jury is made up of twelve individuals who symbolically represent the twelve basic personality fragments, or aspects, of a fully integrated human being as it applies to the original law of the Third-Dimensional Universe. Employing twelve perspectives offers maximum integrated awareness. This awareness is needed to arrive at fair and just evaluations and to determine the appropriate compensation required to restore the balance between individuals, communities, or nations when violations occur.

"The judge who presides within the courtroom *symbolically* represents the higher aspect of the fully integrated human being, the higher self, higher will or state of Godhood. It is the responsibility of the judge to demonstrate wisdom, honor and justice while coordinating and directing activities within the courtroom so that all procedures are executed in truth, impartiality, fairness, and higher reason. Though it may not look that way often enough in your present day system, the original foundation is rooted in ancient divinity."

She looked at me with a powerful intent that riveted our eyes to one another. "Remember, it is not the person, the soul, that is subject to judgment. It is the action or behavior of the person that is to be evaluated. A person's actions may be atrocious, destructive, and needing to be kept in check so that the innocent and the weak may be protected. However, the *being* of a person, the very core essence of the individual, must never be judged as being bad, wrong or evil."

I was captivated by all that she had said, finding it fascinating, even though thoughts of our judicial system conjured up anything but a spiritual process. Nevertheless, I could see that much of the basic process was fair in many, and probably most, of the cases that went to court. But, it was a fact that there was corruption and misuse of the system, although it had diminished over the last few years due to the public exposure of numerous scandals among judicial officials.

"Judgment has its value," I admitted. "We need to judge. But we need to judge fairly and impartially. Assessment, discernment and evaluation seem far more appropriate words to use, since the use of the word judgment has taken on such an unfavorable meaning." I remembered the violations of this last lifetime that I endured.

The memories angered me, and I looked at Divine Mother defiantly, "Well then, how would you evaluate the actions of those barbaric people in that past life, and what they did to Mathias and me? After all, he was just a little boy, and look what they did to him!" I wasn't about to let go of my animosity so easily, even after all I've learned.

Divine Mother paused before answering my question, and instead turned to watch Mathias as he kneeled in a patch of high grass, no doubt studying various crawling things.

"In that life, Mathias was a grown man. He appears to be a little boy to you now, but his soul is just as ancient and eternal as yours." As she continued to watch him, he suddenly leaped to his feet, responding as if she had called out to him, and came running to her side.

They stood facing each other without speaking any words. Her face was radiant as she fondly studied his young, smiling face. They gazed at each other for many moments, not sharing words, but sharing something far deeper than words could express. I could actually feel this non-verbal communication between them, like waves of a sweet, loving vibration that could never be interpreted by any earthly language.

They both turned and faced me, their eyes full and deep, and I basked in their loving gaze, feeling completely accepted in spite of all my shortcomings. My chest filled with warmth, and I knew it was my spiritual heart and soul that responded to the power of love that emanated from Mathias and Divine Mother. I wanted to embrace this awesome power completely, and at the same time I was a little afraid of it.

I watched as their bodies began to waver, then shimmer. The meadow landscape grew fuzzy, and I knew that I was about to embark on another journey of self-discovery. By reason of my last experience, I was not at all looking forward to this. Every muscle in my body seemed to contract and resist.

Divine Mother, Mathias and the meadow disappeared, as a swirl of intense light and sound whisked me away and buffeted me about. I tried to relax, yet my fear of something dreadful to come consumed every thought. What would my lesson be this time?

ELEVEN

The turbulence and noise increased, and I spun un-
controllably, calling out to Divine Mother. I thought
I heard her voice, but the terrible noise grew to such
a frightening pitch that I could not hear her. Fear was in
control and it was impossible for me to think clearly. I
could only think of my safety and of ways to escape this
terror. Anger replaced fear as my spinning and tumbling
seemed like some sadistic harassment from evil forces.

"I don't want to be here!" I strained to be heard over
the ferocious sea of energy as my feet were tossed over my
head repeatedly in a maddening somersault. "Stop! Leave
me alone! I'm not your toy to play with!"

The more I raged on, the worse the assault became.
Over and over, head over heels, heels over head I went. I
had no idea which way was up or down. The more I strug-
gled against the force, the more exhausted I became. Fight-
ing the force only created more confusion and lack of
control. I'm not going to make it if this continues. I can't
last much longer.

The instant I realized that I had no control over the
circumstances, I gave in and surrendered, slowed my
breathing, and focused my attention on my heart-mind
center.

Immediately, the brutal storm quieted and began to
settle into softer waves of shimmering light. Finally the
spinning stopped. Relieved, I relaxed into even greater

trust and calmness. I grew increasingly grateful for the peace that arose. The more centered and grateful I became, the more tranquil the energy. I felt clearer and more alive. Letting out a deep sigh, I thanked God . . . and Divine Mother.

The sea of energy dissipated, giving way to an awesome vista of majestic mountain ranges that stretched far into the distant horizon. Floating high above the summit, my vision was filled with the sight of lush forests, rich with greenery that draped and cascaded over rocky pinnacles and abysmal canyon valleys. A rich vibrancy permeated the air, and the potency of life energy pulsated all around and through me.

The panorama of craggy mountain tops seemed alive with humming radiance, as if the earth itself was buzzing with some mysterious power. Floating closer to the tops of gigantic redwoods, I marveled at the vitality of the vegetation, far deeper and more alive than anything I could remember. These redwoods were colossal in comparison to the giant redwoods I had seen many times during my journeys along the western coast of North America. Where was I? Have I gone back in time once more?

The speed of my descent quickened, and all at once I found myself rocketing toward an open area in the forest. I was propelled silently toward the form of a man standing quietly in the grassy clearing. He seemed to be waiting for something.

As I popped into his body, the soft jolt of the impact brought a sway of disorientation. Looking down at the place where I now stood, I studied the strange body.

Covering my feet and legs were wrappings of animal skin, held in place by straps of thick leather, crisscrossing from the soles. They wound around my legs and ran up to the knees. The furry insides of the boots were warm and cozy, softly cradling my toes and heels in a way that offered a pleasant cushion for walking.

While my leggings were warm and flexible, my upper body was clothed in a shaggy fabric of a rough wool. It was draped over a snug, longsleeved garment. I was dressed to maintain warmth in this cold climate.

As I stood there, I watched wisps of fog as it wafted about on a cool breeze that blew through dew-drenched branches of giant trees. It was early morning, and the bright rising sun began to burn away the crisp chill of the woods.

Dim memories dissolved like dreams as I assumed the identity of this body and became filled with its thoughts and beliefs.

Feeling robust and young, I flexed my arm and shoulder muscles. Reaching up, my fingers raked through a head full of thick, wavy hair that grew down to the tops of my shoulders. As I stared at my large strong hands, I became mesmerized by a wide band of gold on my left ring finger. Artfully crafted upon the shiny metal were clusters of intricate stars, with the crescent moon cradled in the middle. I had vague recollections of the meaning of these symbols, which both intrigued and disturbed me.

The confusion about the ring vanished as my attention was sharply drawn to a magnificent stag that pranced boldly into the sunlight from the darkness of the forest. He came to a sudden halt and froze upon seeing me.

Regaining my senses, I realized that my prayers for an offering of special ceremonial meat had been answered and that I had been blessed by the Great Mother Goddess. As I slowly and smoothly lifted crossbow and arrow to eye level, I gave silent thanks and requested the higher powers to guide the flight of the fatal point to its living mark, to bring a swift and easy death.

I concentrated on the beautiful animal which was standing perfectly still and locking onto me with huge, knowing eyes. Sending my gratitude to the creature with all my heart, I let go of the narrow shaft and heard the fleeting whir of its flight before it struck the stag directly in the heart. He fell instantly with a soft, dull thud.

Approaching him, I laid my hand upon the large vein in his neck, relieved and grateful to feel no pulse; the living force had been snuffed out quickly. I placed my hand on his forehead and thanked the wild spirit that gave his body life, and which in turn would provide the sacred ritual food for holy festivities.

For the meat to retain its highest quality, I performed the usual severing of tendons and removal of bladder and bowels. The body was too large and heavy to carry on my shoulders, so I set about to cut and fashion a carrier from nearby slender, young aspen. I bound the trimmed wooden poles together with leather straps.

Straining and perspiring heavily, I dragged the load behind me. The warm sun was directly overhead when I finally reached the village. I was greeted by a crowd of men who excitedly quit their labors to admire the powerful animal that my arrow had brought down.

They murmured agreeably on hearing my story of the morning and the blessings of the Great Mother Goddess, while others took the body away to prepare it properly for the next day's festival.

An exceedingly fat flask of savory brew was shoved into my hands, and my thirst was soon quenched. I shared the drink with the jovial crowd, and the noise of laughter and friendly bantering grew with each passing 'round of the flask.

The familiar, clear voice of a woman sounded above the mirthful roar,which fell to an abrupt silence upon hearing her words. The crowd made way for her, removing their hats and bowing their heads as Maloa moved toward me with long, sweeping strides.

Our eyes riveted on one another. My delight in

seeing her was mixed with dim foreboding. Uneasiness with Maloa did not seem to make any sense to me, as the flawless beauty of her face and long, shimmering red hair radiated an image of purity and holiness. Her eyes were enormous pools of mysterious knowingness and wisdom.

The spellbinding depth of her eyes induced a momentary shiver of apprehension, but I managed a confident smile when she stopped within arm's length and held out her left hand to me. I grasped her hand eagerly, fell to one knee and kissed the pale softness from the delicate wrist to the tips of her fingers. As my lips lingered on the coolness of her skin, my eyes fell upon the ring she wore, which was a duplicate of mine. Startled, I drew back sharply, gawking at the symbols on the band of gold.

"What is it, Thurion? Already drunk with brew before the morrow's festivities? You seem to have a habit of striving to be the first at everything." Maloa yanked her hand rudely from my grip as nervous laughter arose from several onlookers. "Come to my chambers when you are clearheaded," she snapped, then turned from me to gather her escort of several women.

She glided away on gold-thonged feet which seemed to float above the ground, while her long, silken robe billowed softly with the sway of her hips. I watched her pleasing form move up the path toward the mountain citadel, the Holy Temple, and felt the familiar hunger in my loins.

Teasing remarks from the remaining bystanders brought a flush of heat to my face, but I smiled anyway, casting my face downward with the hope that no one would see the look of scorn in my eyes.

She did this to control me, to keep me within her power. She used whatever method she could to rob me of my prowess and make me the fool among my comrades. Somehow she had me under a spell, and I did not know how to break free from it.

As High Priestess, her powers and wisdom were well respected throughout the land. She could heal the sick and call the dead back to life, if she wanted to. There was no one who could escape Maloa's influence, except perhaps, the old wizardress who lived high in the mighty mountains to the east.

Stories of wicked wars and power struggles between them brought awe and dread to those who listened to the tales of terrible explosions that ripped land and villages apart.

During this time, other powerful women of sorcery began to invade, one by one, from faraway empires. To prove that their powers were mightier, they tried to oust the mountain wizardress and Maloa from their rich territory. Innocent folk were terrorized day and night, never knowing when a knock upon their door meant a visit from a friendly neighbor or a clever sorceress disguised as a poor beggar or as a child seeking shelter.

The stories go on to say that the sorcery wars ended when there came to be far too much destruction and sorrow in the land. Another version tells that the wars ended when the old wizardress and the High Priestess joined forces, discovering that it was far better to be allies than enemies; for together, they were able to force the foreign challengers back to their own domains.

Maloa, the old wizardress, the priestesses, the sorceresses and the wise women were enchantresses, all of them. Beguiling they were to the men who looked into their eyes. It was impossible to avoid the gaze of these supernatural women, as they wielded the power to influence a man's thoughts and desires. In this way Maloa controlled me and any man she wanted. It was the way of all the women.

The women of these lands pledged their homage to Maloa, and stood steadfastly beside her. It was an ancient custom for all infant girls to be brought into the Temple of the High Priestess and reared within the walls of the high court and holy chambers. They received life-long tutelage from the women who were guardians of the ancient holy wisdom.

Women were considered to be daughters of the Mother Goddess and inheritors of the right to use the creative life force power. Maloa was the earthly embodiment of the Mother Goddess and the executor of that power for training future priestesses.

The women were responsible for the education of all the children. Infant boys were also reared in the Temple of the High Priestess, but never in the holy chambers. When the boys became pubescent, they were released to their fathers to learn the ways of men, the hunt and skills of labor; but they were never allowed to learn the ancient holy wisdom taught within the holy chambers.

These boys became men who would perceive the secrecy of women's knowledge with fearful respect and suspicion. This practice ensured that men would remain subservient to women.

The young girls grew into womanhood and became priestesses within the temple and secret gardens. Women were strictly limited in their associations with men. They were permitted to mingle with men for procreative purposes, for brief chaperoned visits, to attend to injuries or illnesses, and during special ritual or holy ceremonies only. All women learned the ways of council, government, healing, divination and enchantment, with most of their time being spent in study or in service.

Sometimes a woman was granted permission to remain with a man of her choice in his dwelling, staying long enough to conceive and give birth to a child so that the infant could cast its eyes upon and know its father.

After that, the mother would return to the temple with her child, as was the custom. The fathers would often endure many weeks and sometimes months of despondency, knowing that they would not see the child again for many years — not until the young boys were old enough, or only during those times when the children were taken beyond the temple walls for excursions throughout the countryside as an extension of their education. The baby girls grew into women who rarely associated with or acknowledged their fathers and were taught that sisterhood among the women, homage to Maloa and the Great Mother Goddess were more important.

The men would yearn for the special attention and conversation as well as the gentle touch and caress that only a woman could offer. The invitation to a long night's stay in a woman's bed chamber was enough to persuade any man to do whatever she would bid. The women were highly skilled in all ways that brought a man's body and soul rich fulfillment, joy and deep contentment.

It was during these intimate times with a woman that a man felt the closest to the Mother Goddess. It was a powerful time for a man; it was his link to the Divine. The women enjoyed the subtle control that they wielded over the men, and resisting Maloa's influence was never a consideration to them, no matter how much the power of the creative life-force was abused.

It was Maloa who was the most powerful and most enchanting of all women. She no doubt kept some secrets to herself which assured that she would maintain her position as High Priestess.

I loved her deeply and passionately, while at the same time I detested her, as did the others. There had been a growing restlessness among the men, and we gathered in the safest of faraway places to share our discontent, but could only do so briefly for fear that Maloa would suspect a plot against her. Some of us fell into guilt about our plotting. For when Maloa was content, there was none more beautiful, none sweeter and kinder than she.

Her generosity was known and appreciated far and wide among the villages of the vast countryside. Compassion and mercy had brought her into the fields of our labor many times when there was widespread drought or pestilence, for she was able to save the precious crops with her invocation of the healing forces of nature.

Maloa blessed the children with her protective powers, and there were never any sick among them. Gold, fine clothing and special attention were given to the fathers of the infants. The best of education was provided in the temple for all children without obligation.

When she was pleased with me, there was none more giving, none more captivating, none more entertaining and loving than she. Maloa was everything. She had the power to do and to have whatever she wanted.

But when she was angry, there was none worse, none more frightening and wicked than Maloa. One never knew what small slight would provoke her into a wrathful tirade, and many an innocent man suffered a painful death as the result of some accidental offense.

Once she evoked the burning of the fields of grain to the ground when she discovered disgruntled gossip about her among the commoners. More than once, she caused torment among the villagers when a man disobeyed her commands or failed to please her in bed.

Our lands were rich in harvest, our children happy and healthy, the forests abundant with wildlife, the rivers forever flowing and the fellowship of dear friends ever present. We had so much to be thankful for. All that we had was provided for us and sustained by Maloa's ability to commune with and command the forces of nature. In order to have all of this good fortune, however, we had to be slaves to her moods. Even the women of her court both loved and feared her.

Her homage was to the great Mother Goddess, and it was from this source that she claimed to receive her wisdom and the powerful ability to use the creative life force. I revered the Mother Goddess as well, praying to her often, and was deeply grateful for Her blessings.

As High Priestess, Maloa did indeed radiate a most holy brilliance at the height of her greatest kindness and compassionate deeds. On these occasions there was no doubt that she was the earthly embodiment of the great Mother Goddess Herself. This was when I loved her, honored and cherished her the most.

Yet, the misuse of the creative life force for selfish and destructive motives was not of the Goddess, this I knew; and it led to confusion and unhappiness among all in the land. There had been increasing distrust and rejection of the Goddess principle itself, which led to blaming the Divine Mother for Maloa's irresponsibility and treachery with this enormous power.

I grew uneasy with these thoughts for fear that Maloa would know, so I would keep them from my awareness. Because of this, I would busy myself, sometimes too much, along with the men. There was always so much to do.

In spite of this, the discontent intensified among the men, growing to raging proportions when one of the most admired of them was rendered into permanent paralysis in his legs when he rebuked Maloa for misuse of the creative life force that gave her such powers.

"This must come to an end!" Venting his hostility, Saber banged the table violently with his fist during our hastily called meeting. He thrust his finger in my direction and bellowed, "You, Thurion, are the only hope we have of stopping this tyrannical rule of power!"

"Me? Why me?" Rising from my chair, I spun around to face the men in the room. "I cannot stand up to such powers. Maloa is much too clever to be fooled by anyone. Even now she knows we are greatly incensed by her latest abomination, and has called me to her court for interrogation. What can one man do against sorcery?"

"You're different. She's in love with you," another man chided in a mocking tone, as some of the men snickered and others grumbled. "Maloa has never treated any man the way she has treated you, Thurion. You have swayed her many times with your charm, saving us from her wrath more than once. And you wear her ring. That is an honor bestowed upon the most beloved. You must be pretty spry betwixt the sheets and the pillows!" he cackled gleefully as the others roared with laughter, some rolling their eyes and slapping their thighs.

"All right! You've had your fun at my expense." Feeling the blush in my face, I forced a weak grin. "What is it that you expect me to do?" Glancing down at the ring, I felt some dismay at being so deceptive with Maloa. Betraying a sacred trust is punishable by death. Even if I were able to cloak my real motives from her, I could not hide the invading darkness that caused an uneasiness in my chest.

Old Enki, one of the most respected of the elders, spoke with a crackle in his voice, "Convince her that she is misusing the Power. Convince her that she is out of integrity with the highest interest of the Goddess. Increasing numbers of our countrymen are outraged and are renouncing the Goddess as a guiding force in their lives. Tell her that by the example she sets, she is encouraging the women of her own courts to misuse the power as well."

With a rasping tone, he went on, "This is a serious matter, since there has been desperate talk in recent years among those who have left their faraway lands to escape the mighty ones in those places who are abusing the Power as well. It can be said with certainty that the scales of power have been weighted heavily and unfairly on the side of women for too long. We must render Maloa, and all other women, powerless before each one of us is consumed. Let us rebuke the Goddess and deliver to us the God of men! Let us rekindle Jove, Zeus, mighty Thor and Abcah." The rage of the men increased as a result of his words. They shouted and clamored even more loudly than before.

Rebuke the Goddess? This is madness, I realized, as hostility blazed in the eyes of all in the room. I was witnessing the eruption of ancient rage that had been suppressed for more than a thousand years. The silent frustrations of living under the control of powerful women had been passed from father to son for countless generations. What could I do? I was caught in between.

"Thurion, you must help us," pleaded Ilia, my closest friend. "You alone can do this. Persuade her in our favor with your own pleasing manner, and we will not have to resort to force or violence. Think of the lives you will save. You must do this for us, and for the welfare of all the people."

I hung my head in despair, feeling the swarm of confusion in my mind. It seemed a long while before I could open my mouth, and I spoke weakly. "Then . . . let it be so. I will do as you ask."

The men cheered and rushed to me, the bulk of them gratefully slapping me on the back. I was not pleased with my decision, yet knew that words of truth were spoken on this day.

Something was happening in the land both near and far away. Some disturbing element was descending upon this world like the smothering, damp thickness that permeates the air before the outbreak of a dangerous winter storm.

Eventually, I was able to get away from the men as they wallowed in their discontentment, growing to excessive drunkenness with their prized brew. I needed to be alone before I met with Maloa at the appointed time.

I ran along the path that led back to the village and on to Maloa's High Court. Running would help ease the tension, and if I ran all the way I would find myself in better spirits. The sun was sinking fast in the afternoon sky, and the shadows of towering trees stretched across the path, shading my way with a refreshing coolness as I pushed my legs to their limit.

My thoughts raced and I tried to force guilt from my mind, knowing that Maloa would sense this and question me. By the time I reached the citadel gates, I was bathed in sweat and gasping for breath. Sitting down to rest, I considered carefully how I might speak to Maloa. I rehearsed several conversations in silence and practiced calming my mind, feeling certain that I could shield my intention. However, with Maloa's powerful abilities, it would be difficult.

Finally, I arose and faced the giant iron gates, and sent a prayer to the great Mother Goddess. I begged for Her protection. I prayed that the Goddess would guide my speech and open Maloa's heart to compassion so that she could hear the truth and change her ways. The presence and blessings of the Divine Mother filled my heart with courage and peace, and I was lost in a few moments of bliss.

My reverie was broken by the clanking of heavy metal. Looking up, I saw two women slowly opening the gates. The great hinges groaned and creaked as the sides swung inward toward the courtyard. "You are expected, Thurion." A third woman, Ina, approached gracefully, gesturing me to follow her.

Remembering my frequent visits to Maloa's court, I cast an appreciative glance across the familiar marble floors and the white stone pillars that towered into domed cathedral ceilings. The high, broad windows allowed rays of cheerful sunlight to shine upon vibrant indoor gardens. Even the most harried of souls could find peace in this place, with its alluring fragrance and the faint echoes of soft flute and harp music.

My name was announced, and I was ushered into Maloa's personal bed chamber. It was far more than a bed chamber; it was her place of quiet refuge, and was filled with fresh flowers and a scent of cinnamon and vanilla. A warming blaze crackled and popped on the stone hearth. Fine wine and exquisitely prepared foods were arranged attractively upon a round myrtlewood table.

There sat Maloa, smiling radiantly, her regal image framed within a large peacock chair. She arose quickly and threw her arms about my neck. Our lips touched, and a long, passionate kiss dissolved, for the moment, all of my concerns.

She drew back suddenly, searching me deeply with her hauntingly beautiful eyes and asked, "So, my beloved, what are the men so unhappy about?" She let go of me, almost pushing me away, and began stalking about the room. "They seem angry, and I don't like it. Their hostility hovers over the land like vulgar sludge. I can feel it and so can the others. Tell me, Thurion, what is going on?"

Composing myself and shielding my feelings and thoughts with all the power I had, I breathed slowly, not giving in to nervousness. "Maloa . . . Maloa, my precious High Priestess, my charming Goddess, my only love . . . the men are simply a little concerned with some things that are difficult for them to understand. They are restless. There has been some talk, only rumors mind you, of renouncing the Holy Mother Goddess."

"What?" Maloa's eyes became wide with alarm. "It's impossible to renounce the Goddess! She is everything.

146

She is the earth, the food upon their plates, the crops growing in their fields, the trees in the forest, the animals, the clouds in the sky, the birthing of their children. Without the Goddess, they would not live! How can they consider such a thing?" She flung her arms about and paced furiously back and forth, her flowing white satin robe reflected in the polished marble floor.

She ranted on and on, then stopped short. "It's about Thayer, isn't it?" Her piercing gaze was penetrating. I managed to remain unmoved. Annoyed with my unresponsiveness, she shouted, "Thayer provoked me! He provoked me into rendering him paralyzed. I would not have done so if it were not true!"

I gritted my teeth in contempt and felt the flush of rage rush into my face. "Maloa! You did not have to punish him so cruelly because he disagreed with you. It's wrong to use the Power this way. The Mother Goddess would not use the creative life force power to avenge such pettiness. There have been far too many of these over-reactive and irrational responses, Maloa. The people are losing their faith in you, and they are blaming the Goddess for your irresponsibility!" Finally, I let loose my fury and disclosed what I had hoped to conceal.

She glared at me hatefully, with a vicious, inhuman intensity I had never before witnessed; and I found myself staring into the transformed face of a horrible demon-animal. I froze, not knowing if she would strike me dead or torture me with a horrid curse of revenge.

She hissed bitterly through clenched teeth, "It is not the people who lose their faith in me or the Goddess. It is only the men who do so. It is the men who want to bring the Goddess down and erect a foolish phallic symbol in Her place!" Maloa's fist slammed the tabletop, electrifying the atmosphere with her seething fury.

Then unexpectedly, her raging mood broke, and she

dropped into the great peacock chair, buried her head in her hands, and sobbed pitifully. This behavior was unfamiliar to me — the much feared and all-powerful Maloa had become reduced to a sniveling child right before my eyes. I softened, regretting the animosity I had held toward her, and bent over and caressed her shoulders.

"Maloa, my beloved, what is it? What is this that is happening to you?" Stroking and kissing her long, lustrous hair seemed to calm her, and she raised her head slowly, brushing the tears from her face.

"Thurion, please sit down. I have something to tell you." She pointed to another chair, and I brought it close beside her.

"I am ready to listen, my Goddess. Always I am here when you are in need of me." I felt close to her, knowing that she needed my strength in this moment of her weakness. I held her hand tenderly.

"For a long, long time, I have known that the downfall of the Goddess was coming," Maloa admitted. "Hathia, the old wizardress in the mountains, has never been wrong in her prophecies. She and I have become friends because we understand one another's position during these times of great change." Maloa looked off across the room and out of the window, seeming to be a great distance away in her thoughts as she went on.

"Hathia and I laugh when we recall how her envy of me and the lush lands under my domain provoked the war that nearly destroyed us all and ruined the beautiful land. We eventually came to our senses, and we ceased our power struggle.

"Of course, when we became allies, we used our powers to restore the villages and countryside to even greater beauty and richness than ever before. That era was the most peaceful, prosperous and abundant time on the face of the earth. There was contentment and joy throughout the lands."

She spoke wistfully, regretting that those times were past. "All people seemed happier. All people, including the men, were satisfied with the balance of power, although I suppose some never quite forgot nor forgave Hathia and me for the turmoil. Perhaps they use this event of the past as an added reason to overthrow our rule.

"We have felt the encroachment of the new thought, the new belief in the land; and with each generation it has grown darker and more dismal. The prophecies of Hathia foretell that all men, all women, and all children will come under the control and influence of distorted and wounded masculine and patriarchal thinking.

"Women will become sadly submissive and will be dominated by the power of men's excessive use of logic and by their dangerous, aggressive behavior. Women will lose their power, their faith and unity with the Goddess. They will become subservient to men in almost every way. The only respected realm left to women will be birthing, child-rearing, and taking care of others."

More tears welled up in Maloa's eyes as she spoke: "With the rise of the wounded and angry patriarchy will come the thoughtless destroying and abuse of our precious earth and the beloved animals. Women and even innocent children will be horribly abused."

She sighed heavily, feeling great remorse. "There will be countless wars and much suffering. There will be strange illnesses that cannot be cured, and there will be an irreverence about foods that are taken into the body, which will have tragic impact on the people and will generate severe mental, emotional, physical, and spiritual diseases.

"The people will come to worship a form of coinage and strive to accumulate as much of it as they can, fostering the illusion of security that they believe will come from it. How much of this coinage they collect and spend will determine the measure of their worth. They will no longer find personal worth and value in the divinity within themselves and their connectedness with all of life.

"The people will forget the Goddess and will deny their connection with nature. They will pay homage to a false and vengeful god. Hathia says there is nothing we can do to stop this from happening. She thought that we could, at least, delay the unfolding of events by increasing our control over men." She looked at me mournfully.

"So . . . that is why you have become so unyielding over these recent years! You have been afraid. You have been afraid of every man's disagreement or resistance because you saw these behaviors as a sign of things to come — when the men would take control." I was dumbfounded. We sat in silence, deeply disturbed about the future.

Maloa spoke, almost in a whisper, "And . . . men and women will never fully trust each other, Thurion, not for a very long time. Men and women will always be highly attracted to one another. But there will be millenniums of distrust, rage, grievance, betrayal, shame, guilt, and denial influencing the relationship of every man and woman.

"Instead of being attracted to one another to create greater joy and spiritual union together, men and women will be strongly attracted to one another through unhealthy dependencies. Men and women who have unconsciously chosen to shut themselves off from these ancient wounds will be irresistibly drawn to the very person that will bring these painful issues to the surface.

"Through these powerful attractions, men and women will succumb to the compulsive desire to work through power struggles and battles associated with the subconscious memories of ancient wounds. And all these wounds will remain hidden inside each individual until the appropriate partner arrives to trigger the memories.

"The patriarchy will govern the thinking of men and women for a long time," she said, seeming to labor with each word. "Just as the men hate me and rise up against me, so they will rise up against all women and all things associated with the feminine, until the painful subconscious memories of the betrayal, abandonment, control and domination are healed."

Swallowing hard and holding back the flood of emotion, I asked, "How has all of this come about? What started this madness?"

"A very long time ago," Maloa responded, "only a few men were envious of the power of women. Most were content and satisfied with the way things were; most did not want the enormous responsibilities that women had. They were happy with their simpler lives. The very few rebellious ones made little or no impact on the thinking of men.

"Over time, there came to be greater discontentment. I do not know the reason why these things came about, only that some of these discontented ones were simply not happy with themselves and wanted more than what our cultural philosophies and customs offered.

"These unhappy ones blamed women for having too much control, taking attention away from men and stifling their freedom. It may seem hard to believe that such things could instigate this unrest. But careful researching of these ideas has provided some understanding.

"Those who receive the greater portion of attention will have the greater degree of power. Energy will always follow the strongest flow of attention, and the greater portion of power will reside in that field." She paused to stare out of the window at the starry dusk and crescent moon that dangled low in the sky. Lighting the candles one by one upon the table, Maloa went on speaking as the candlelight shimmered in her moist eyes.

"If a man is unhappy with himself, if he is unfulfilled in his work and with events in his life, he may become envious of someone who appears to have more power or control than he. In particular, he may be envious of women who are in positions of power, and who receive a great deal of attention.

"Little by little, a man of this nature may demonstrate disrespect for such women out of jealousy, which is a projection of the dissatisfaction and lack he feels within himself. Because it may be too uncomfortable for such a man to accept responsibility for his own unhappiness, he will resort to blaming women for taking attention and happiness away from him. The game gains momentum when a man seeks out various ways to take power from women to force the energy to come his way.

"When a man attempts to take power from a woman, it takes the form of putting her down, criticizing her and showing disrespect. He may minimize the importance of her accomplishments and fall into abusive forms of behavior on the emotional, mental and physical levels. Sometimes he will do this aggressively and violently, sometimes through secretive manipulations and passive behavior for the purpose of maintaining control."

She glanced downward as a look of shame washed across her face. "The raping of women will also be one of many methods used to ensure the domination and control over women and to keep them in fear."

Then she looked up into my eyes with great sadness. "There will be rejection of sacred sexuality, and intercourse will be reduced to mere physical gratification, an urge to be satisfied, which will eliminate that pathway of holy union with the Goddess. People will be taught to be ashamed of their bodies, and new religions will convince the people that sexual union is for procreation only and that it is not holy to enjoy this act of intimacy.

"It will be considered wicked for a woman to find

pleasure in sexual encounters with a man. Ancient unconscious memories will cause men to be suspicious of a woman who is sexually wise and sensual and who finds joy in her sexual expression. Such women will come to be regarded as unwholesome, and will be given the names of whore and prostitute. Society will look upon them with disdain. This fear and uneasiness with such women will remain for a long time, perpetuated by unconscious memories of a time when women wielded power over men through sexual prowess and by limiting access to the creative life force through sexuality.

"With such fearful and unhealthy judgments abounding, women will become frigid and dissociated from the Goddess. They will come to deny the sensuousness of their own bodies. They will learn to mistrust their ability to experience the power and natural joyful fulfillment of sexual union. They will forget the unity with the divine which it once brought to both men and women.

"The new religions will be led by men who fear and refuse to acknowledge the Goddess. They will trust and praise only those women who remain subservient, obedient, and submissive.

"Influenced by the unconscious memories of ancient pain, men will strive adamantly to maintain dominion and control in order to prevent women and the Goddess from ever gaining power again. Both men and women will suffer greatly because of the distorted rule of the patriarchy.

"As women give up their power and unity with the Goddess, they will become weak and will develop an unhealthy dependency upon men. Not wanting to be abandoned or to lose the protection and security provided by men, women will become overly compliant and subservient to ensure that men will continue to protect and take care of them.

"Women will cease to be authentic thinkers and will become weak in their use of wise, objective discernment and natural intuition. This will cause them to fall into patterns of irrational and overly emotional behavior, further weakening their powers of perception. In this way, women will remain in subservient roles and submissive behavior through hundreds of generations. This is how the Goddess will be overthrown.

"Even though men will succeed in achieving dominance in the world, there will come a time, a very long time ahead in the future, when men will realize that their hearts are empty, their lives dry and void of inspiration and meaningful creativity. They will come to recognize that the accumulation of possessions, the winning of wars, the building of sterile empires, and the controlling and domination of others, cannot quell the deep, eternal yearning for peace and love in their souls.

"Women, too, will discover that their resentment and rage, suppressed for thousands of years, will also need healing before their hearts can be filled once more with love.

"All in all, the wounds that men and women have afflicted upon one another will only be healed through the letting go of the need to blame each other for the deep soul pain suffered throughout earth's history." With this last statement, Maloa sank into a chasm of despondency.

All that she spoke of brought images of a world where chaos reigned, and these images troubled me deeply. I thought long about it. Gently squeezing Maloa's delicate hand, I asked her, "Maloa . . . could it be . . . that this all began because men simply want to be free?"

"What do you mean?" she raised her head in surprise. "Are the men not free to enjoy all that they have? They are free to enjoy more than enough food for their tables. They have handsome homes, and their fields are more than abundant with healthy crops. Their children are happy, well-educated and radiant. The men are well-provided for. What greater freedom than that do the men want?" Maloa was truly incredulous with the idea.

"Maloa, I believe that men want to have greater freedom to express themselves." I said, pausing for her response.

"Do you mean to express their desire to overthrow the Goddess? I cannot permit that, Thurion. Is that the freedom you speak of? I shall have none of it!" she blurted out, jerking her hand away and raising her head defiantly.

I felt a wave of pain from Maloa, and I chose my next words carefully. "The intention to overthrow the Goddess is only the result of the pain felt by many generations of men who have been forced to deny and suppress their own needs and desires. Men want to explore and create everything their minds can fathom. They want adventure. They want to go beyond the limitations that have been placed upon them through women's philosophies and ancient customs. They desire the education, knowledge and power that women have, but which men are not allowed to have according to tradition. They want to have more time and interactions with the women and their children. Women have withheld from men the ancient wisdoms.

"Men have been controlled, smothered and enslaved because women have misused the life force power. Men have been powerless to control even their own bodies and have been manipulated through women's prowess with sexual energy; this you already know. Maloa, the men want to have more power and greater freedom."

"Men will never achieve freedom by conquering women, Thurion," Maloa snapped, teary-eyed and furious. She then became thoughtful and quiet. The silence was long and heavy.

155

After a while, she spoke, with a tone of defeat in her voice. "I know what you say is true." Her words were slow to come. "The women have controlled men to a great degree. However, it seems as though men believe they will have freedom when women are subdued and made powerless. I see that this will generate an impasse of great duration.

"Neither men nor women will be able to negotiate as equals for a long time to come. I realize that I, and all women, have reacted to the changing behaviors in men with fear and resistance. Rather than working through the differences between men and the women, we have amplified the very behavior that men want to end. But it is too late now, Thurion." She hung her head, leaned against the palm of her hand and rested upon the table, as if a thousand years of hopelessness saturated her entire being.

"The enormity of this vengeful movement in the minds of men is so vast that any reversal of my behavior or that of any other woman, will not solve the problem," she added, "for it has gone on too long. The men will achieve their dominion over the women through the power of their growing numbers. The multitudes have produced mass beliefs that have become increasingly powerful— far more powerful than any sorceress can defeat. Because women have experienced fear for the first time, that fear alone will dissipate any power we have left.

"Women will become fragmented and will no longer stand beside one another. Women will lose faith in the power of the feminine, and will distrust each other. It will be far in the future before women begin to come together for the purpose of healing themselves and the world. Yet, before the healing can be achieved, the women will need to deal with their renouncement of the Goddess. Women will need to clear their wounded hearts of the anger, resentment and hurt of painful ancient times. Men will also need to

156

heal their anger, resentment and hurt as well." Maloa fell against the back of her chair with a vacant look in her eyes.

I was deeply moved by all that she had said. Gazing upon her from a renewed perspective, I pulled her toward me and drew her into my arms. She fell limp into my embrace, as though all life had drained from her. Feeling the ache in my heart, I sobbed and clutched her tightly as she wept softly against my chest.

After a little while, she began to kiss me gently on the cheek. Her lips glided sensuously across my neck, feather-soft, and I shivered at the moist stroke of her tongue. Into my ear she seductively whispered the alluring, stirring, sacred words of the secret ancient language, touching lightly upon my groin, my heart, then my forehead. A surge of arousal swelled within me, and, gathering her long hair into my grasp, I pulled her head back sharply and placed my mouth upon hers.

Sensitive and vibrant hands touched, squeezed, caressed, and embraced every sensuous place, as layer upon layer of clothing dropped to the floor about our feet. When the last remnant fell away, I eagerly swept Maloa into my arms and lifted her to her bed, the union of our eyes never broken.

All sadness and doubts subsided as we playfully engaged in the sweet seduction of our souls. Drawn into the abyss of dizzying passion, our naked bodies quivered joyously, pulsing with the wondrous power of the life force. Timelessness prevailed, and infinite oneness was ours for an explosive moment of divine ecstasy as these, our mortal bodies, trembled in holy union.

Blissfully spent and breathless, we tenderly whispered our gratitude for the blessings of the Holy Mother Goddess; and tears of contentment glistened in Maloa's eyes. I cradled her in my arms as we lay quietly, my body and soul in exquisite peace.

I longed to stay in this peace, this bliss, forever. I wanted Maloa with me always just as she was with me now, so very soft, so much in surrender to me, although I knew it would not last. After these thoughts passed, I finally drifted into pleasant sleep.

Much later, I was awakened by a strange sound at the door, and I raised my head to peer into the darkness. The fire had gone out and the last candle burned down to a soft, glowing ember. All about the room was black against a deeper blackness. Perhaps I did not hear anything, or maybe it was only the settling of the thick walls of heavy stone. Complacent, I laid back restfully, gently pressing Maloa's warm and slender body against my own.

Suddenly, a flurry of dark, hooded forms burst into the room like a blast of winter wind. They rushed toward us, and before I could rise to face the intruders, forceful hands clutched my body and violently ripped me from Maloa's arms. Her cry was muffled by a hand across her mouth, and I bellowed in raging fury while my body strained against the hold of men. A blow to my head brought instant darkness, and I remembered nothing more.

When I awoke, the throb in my head was excruciating, making it an effort to open my eyes. I could hear voices, and when I was able to look about me, Ilia and several of the men were sitting about his table. Realizing I was in

Ilia's dwelling, memories returned and jolted me to full awareness.

"Maloa, where is Maloa?" I demanded, clenching my jaw, only to wince with the sudden pain in my head. "What have you done with her?"

No one replied. There was only a thick silence, which weighed heavily upon me. I dreaded the obvious answer. All I could do was hold my aching head in my hands and let the tears form in my eyes. I knew then what they had done with her.

"You lied to me. You set me up and used me!" I growled hatefully as the tightness in my chest became unbearable. Scrambling to my feet, I stumbled outside, swaying with dizziness.

Looking out above the trees, I saw the mountain citadel, the temple and high court in flames. Billowing grey smoke spewed out of every window, every opening. The cloud of rising haze blanketed the morning sun and cast a foreboding shadow across the land. As I heard the screaming and shouting of many voices in the distance, I tried not to think about the dark, chaotic days ahead.

Turning to the men seated silently around the table, I pleaded, "Why? Why did you do this? I spoke with Maloa as you asked. She was beginning to understand and may have changed her ways. You didn't need to resort to such violence. And you took her when she was the most vulnerable! You knew her powers were the weakest during the hours of sleep, particularly after . . . after we . . ."

"After she had opened herself to you?" Ilia coldly interjected. "Yes, we knew that she would be the least protected and least wary at that time. For her to have given you the twin of her sacred ring meant that she would drop her protective shields in your presence." His lips twisted into a crooked smirk. "Especially during those intimate moments when the two of you — "

"Stop! You are unbelievably cruel! The sight of all of you sickens me. You have no idea what this means to all of us, to the world and the future . . . " My voice trailed off, knowing that the words I wanted to speak would fall on uncaring ears.

"We stayed with you, Thurion, because we care about our brother." Ilia hung his head as he spoke. "We did not wish to harm you, but we knew that you would put up quite a struggle, and that it would be more merciful if you did not know the full range of our plans."

I could only look at him in disdain, outraged at his lack of remorse. All of them were distant, cold, and unfeeling. Storming out of the door, and knowing I would never return, I ran toward the temple.

The dizziness subsided, yet my head throbbed with pain and guilt. Running as fast as I could, I reached the opened gates of the high court and stopped, gasping for breath.

I could only watch helplessly as the monolithic structure heaved and groaned, the massive columns collapsing inside, one by one. No longer considering life to be worth living, I bolted inside. Blinded by smoke and slapped by searing flames, I cursed and screamed, not caring to save myself from the blaze that began to burn my clothing and my hair. The last colossal pillar gave way, and a mighty sound exploded high above, sending an enormous avalanche of scorched marble and stone upon me.

The deafening thunder of falling debris was all I remembered before floating effortlessly upward like fine mist above the smoky scene. Looking out, I could see the crisp, clear panorama of the craggy mountain range to the east, and all the lands in every direction.

Casting my gaze downward, I could see the streams of smoke emerging from the rubble of the temple. From this great height, it seemed to be a mere miniature version of what existed before. I looked upward, and saw a radiant light. It beckoned me into its soothing brilliance. Reaching out for it gladly, I found myself enveloped in a comforting presence, as a swirl of cool, refreshing wind whipped about me.

Sparkling white was all that was visible, bringing peace and serenity as weariness ebbed away. Relaxing, I became aware of resting on something solid. I realized that I was once again in the meadow, watching the tops of tall trees swaying lazily with the breeze.

TWELVE

I t took longer this time for me to regain my senses. This last life was all-consuming, and the remainder of Thurion's persona squelched total recollection of myself as Clarion. I had truly been lost in that life, completely absorbed in it. As I lay here I wondered, Who was I . . . really? Thurion was every bit as real as Clarion lying here on the grass. Which reality was happening now? That lifetime seemed just as present, just as "now" as *this* "now" that I was experiencing in the meadow.

"Everything is happening now, Clarion. It is your beliefs, perceptions and assumptions that create your interpretations of life events, and your experience of past lives. The passing of time is merely the result of where you place the major focus of your attention." Divine Mother spoke intently.

Sitting up and grinning the biggest grin manageable, I was elated to see her. The import of her words was too much for me at this point   I could not focus enough to respond to her. Still overwhelmed with this last life, my confusion tumbled out in a seemingly endless stream of questions: "Women and men need to heal themselves, don't they? Do you think it all began in that lifetime? Where was I, and what time period was that? Is that why men and women act the way they do toward each other today? Could it be that − "

"Clarion, wait . . . " Muffling soft laughter with her hand, she coaxed me into acknowledging my own experience. "Tell me what you learned. After that, I will share some insight with you."

I paused, realizing that I had learned so much. Where could I begin?

"Well . . . what I remembered most from my experience was a sense of betrayal and guilt and many strong feelings and emotions. All of it was so intense. It was too much, as if I was controlled and consumed by my feelings. I couldn't believe those men could do what they did. It was terrible. And Maloa . . . oh, she was awesome, so beautiful, and so very powerful!" My heart grew heavy with remorse as I recalled the events.

Divine Mother responded, "Your experience was more intense because you were more aware of real feelings. That is how emotions were experienced in those days of long ago. Both men and women were in the powerful flow of all feelings and emotion. The expression of feeling and emotion was considered natural and acceptable.

"However, women achieved greater comfort with the power inherent in emotional energy. Women were — and still are — a more direct reflection of the inner nature, the powerful realm of feelings, where intuition, psychic abilities and union with Spirit are achieved. This was expressed through the acknowledgment of oneness and relationship with all living things of creation . . . the 'We Are' perspective. It is the domain of the Goddess, the feminine expression of the Beloved Creator. Women learned to use this enormous power to command the forces of nature, to foretell the future, and to perform miracles; and they eventually misused the power to manipulate and control men.

"Men did not achieve genuine comfort with the power of feelings and emotions in the same way that women did. Then as well as now, men are a more direct reflection of the outer nature, the realm of logic, analysis, intellect, and the expression of self as a separate individual . . . the 'I Am' perspective. This is the domain of God, the masculine expression of the Beloved Creator. Men learned to use this power to control and manipulate nature and the environment, and to build a progressive world of science and technology. Men eventually misued their abilities by going to extremes. They nearly annihilated the world of nature and over-emphasized individuality, which initiated their separation from the original state of unity with One."

As she spoke, I looked into her radiant face and beheld the healing power of her love. All my sadness and bodily weaknesses were washed away. My eyes searched for Mathias, but he was nowhere to be seen.

"Divine Mother . . . " I began, weighing my words carefully, "men and women have been battling for years, trying to achieve some peace and balance. But this enormous gap of misunderstanding between them only seems to continue. I have watched women become more self-reliant and more independent, achieving leadership in areas that used to be reserved for men. Women are happier with themselves in the realms of self-expression, creativity, and self-empowerment; and yet their satisfaction within relationships has not significantly increased.

"Many men find it difficult to relate to women who are self-confident and powerful. It makes them feel uneasy, and often they become competitive and vindictive toward such women, particularly when they are in positions of leadership."

"Women who have grown beyond being dependent on a man, or who have chosen to be self-reliant instead of subservient, often have difficulty making their way in a world where the higher paying positions of power and influence are largely dominated by men. These empowered women often have more difficulty creating lasting relationships since many men feel intimidated by confident and successful women. These men distrust powerful women, fearing that they will control them or smother their sense of individualtiy.

"On the other hand, women distrust men, fearing that men will rob them of their power, either by force or by withdrawing their emotional and financial support. What can we do to heal this rift between men and women, so that we can truly learn to respect and appreciate each other?"

Divine Mother strolled about, her feet hardly disturbing the grass as she walked. She bent gracefully to pick a few delicate wild flowers and brought them close to her nose. I wondered if she was going to answer my question. As I was about to repeat it, she turned toward me and spoke.

"The unconscious, that is, the hidden aspect within each person, moves us toward healing by creating and re-enacting unresolved, emotionally charged patterns from other lifetimes. These dramas are dressed with the props and surroundings of present circumstances, but the patterns themselves are the same. What this means is that the root cause of an emotionally charged event between a man and a woman has its beginnings in antiquity. It is created because of our compelling desire to play out the intensity of the emotions associated with old wounds. This process continues until the original event is finally healed, through the application of love and forgiveness.

"Each time a man or woman projects anger, discontentment and pain onto the other through blame, hurtful words or actions, it is an unconscious attempt to clear the past injustices and to balance the scales of karma once and for all. Through the events that are recreated over and over again the opportunity is offered to consciously choose more loving behavior.

"Each unpleasant experience, each argument, each

violent act that occurs between a man and a woman carries within it the potential to move beyond the hurt into authentic forgiveness, and to return to love again.

"You choose your response in any situation, in any event. You choose! Will you continue to cling to your need to be right in all disagreements? Will you go on with the need to be in control and to manipulate others into behaving the way you want them to behave so that you can have it your way? Will you continue to give so much emphasis to having dominion in your relationships that you eventually strip away all remnants of love and compassion? Or will you choose to move into the higher aspect, the heart-mind awareness, and know these events as opportunities to heal old wounds and to let love enter in?

"Within each disagreement lies an opportunity to achieve clarity and peace of mind, if you are consciously able to stop the projection of hurt and blame onto others. Will you choose to do this, and to begin taking personal responsibility for your own feelings — your anger, and discontnent, and pain?

Her questions brought to mind countless occasions when I had blamed someone else for making me angry, unhappy, or unfortunate. I wasn't about to take the rap for my own feelings and behavior during those times, because I found it was much easier to blame someone else for my troubles. I observed these same attitudes and perceptions occurring in relationships on all levels: men and women tend to blame each other for the things that go wrong in their lives.

Divine Mother thrust her arm high over her head, fingers stretched wide, and an orange suddenly popped out of nowhere into the palm of her hand. Speechless, I stared as she pulled the orange apart and squeezed it. The juice flowed freely like water, falling quietly onto the grass below.

"How did you do that?" I exclaimed in astonishment, then realized that it was absurd to ask, considering everything I had experienced so far.

"Would you say," Divine Mother asked, "that no matter how the orange is sliced or squeezed, what comes out will always be orange juice?" She paused, giving me time to consider.

"Certainly. What are you getting at?"

As the remainder of the orange dissolved from her hand, the atmosphere about her became quite still. I had come to know how much she enjoyed these opportunities to keep me dangling in an air of suspense.

Breaking the silence, she continued, "When a man or woman becomes angry, sad, upset, disappointed, or dissatisfied in any way, that feeling or attitude is exactly what's inside that person, no matter what another person *appears* to be doing to them. In other words, no matter what one person does to another, no matter how they might "squeeze" another, the feeling, the attitude, the "juice" that emerges in response to an event is a *chosen* response based on what already exists inside that person. So it is futile for men and women to blame each other for their troubles in life or to blame the opposite sex for the troubles in the world.

"Everyone on earth is entirely responsible for their own responses to the conditions and events in their life. Each of you in your own way impacts the world condition through the way you respond and the attitude that you choose in any given moment.

"Although there is greater awareness of the need for healing among the men and women of the world, there is still much rage, resentment, grief and hurt that needs to be healed. There is still a great amount of distrust between the sexes. Men and women continue to carry wounds which influence their interactions with one another on many levels. These wounds create fear and suspicion, as well as relationships and marriages driven by the struggle for power and control.

"Even though many men deny their anger toward women, their unconscious feelings of resentment and fear are often demonstrated in the great variety of strategies through which they attempt to exercise control over women. It can be seen in the manner in which men relate to their wives, mothers, lovers, friends, co-workers, as well as to women in positions of leadership and authority."

After Divine Mother finished this last sentence, I began to wonder why this attitude toward women had gone on for so long. I remembered countless situations in which I witnessed women interacting with men in ways that actually reinforced their oppression.

"Divine Mother," I said, "I have observed many women giving up their power to men so often that I can't help but believe that women have been partly responsible for being in such oppressed and subservient positions. Men have been blamed for creating all the ills and destruction in the world, and I was glad to hear you imply that it can't be the fault of men entirely— that we are all responsible. But there must be something happening on a deeper level that locks many women and men in the same positions of struggle over and over again with very little resolution."

Nodding, she responded, "Allow yourself to understand that women have been in subservient roles for thousands of years and that it is taking some time for them to reawaken and reclaim their true power. Some women do not want to reclaim their power, so they behave in ways that invite or coerce a man to take care of them. Many women fear they will lose the love, attention and material security supplied by their mate, or men in general, if they become more independent and self-reliant.

"Many women fear the responsibilities that come with reclaiming more of their power, and they remain out of touch with the real issues of life on a much deeper level. In these ways, women have indirectly contributed to male domination in your world. Because they do not want to grow and evolve beyond their fear, or to take more responsibility for their lives, many women actually contribute to the patriarchal dominion by taking little or no action at all to set things right.

"Unfortunately, many women ignore the calling from deep within their own soul, and ignore their dreams and desires. Instead, they use their creative energy to bolster a man's visions and goals, often enduring unfullfilling marriages and relationships for the security that the man can provide. In truth, what most women really want is to be free to be themselves and to be more in charge of their lives.

"Listen closely to the conversations among many women with regard to men. Their dialogue abounds with angry criticisms and verbal attacks, accusing men of being responsible for all the problems of the world and for the discontent in their personal lives.

"What these women fail to realize is that they are promoting exactly what they claim they don't want to experience in men. They actually energize the unwanted conditions by focusing enormous amounts of attention and emotional intensity on the undesirable behavior. This only serves to aggravate the situation and supports the continuing manifestations of these behaviors.

"To put it another way, all of you experience your strongest beliefs wherever you are. The more you focus upon an idea and support it with the belief that it represents reality, then you will experience that reality.

"If women want men to treat them with greater kindness and respect, then women must stop being attracted to men who are unkind to them. If women are outraged by runaway consumption in the world, by overemphasis on material success, by excessive accumulation of possessions and misuse of natural resources, then they must stop being attracted to the kind of man whose sense of personal power comes from his bank account and how many things he can buy and accumulate. Women must gather their courage and raise their voices to bring attention to the manipulation and harming of the environment, and to any mistreatment of children and animals.

"If women want a peaceful and beautiful world, then women must take a stand for what they believe in and make positive changes in themselves first. The peace, love, joy and goodwill that women want in their lives, in their families, and for the children of the world will never come about if they wait for the men to make these changes.

"Women can become the leaders in this area through the example they set, and by making courageous changes in their own lives and attitudes, within their families, and within the community at large.

"The world will not be at peace until both men and women achieve peace with each other and within themselves as individuals. It is time for the women to reunite with one another under the guidance and power of the Goddess. In order for your beloved earth and humanity to experience wholeness once more, women must remember their original divine sisterhood, and men must remember their original divine brotherhood."

Divine Mother's words touched me at a very deep level, and for a time I was unable to speak. I felt my own frustration with all the ways that have kept men and women so locked into disappointment, anger, and blame.

I remembered my lifetime with Maloa and the words she spoke about the demise of sacred sexuality. Even though we, as a burgeoning race, have just barely entered into the new millennium with greater maturity, sex remains a touchy topic in most of the world.

I recalled my experience with Maloa and the intensity of sexual arousal, a foreign sensation to this aging body of mine. In that lifetime, the sexual feelings felt natural and powerful, almost mystical— although in those moments when passion grew intense, I was aware of the submerging of reason, and the dismissal of the intellect. It disturbed me to lose that much control over myself.

Many people today are frightened of losing control, of surrendering to the full power of passion. We are afraid we will look foolish, or that we might be hurt in some way. We are afraid that if we give up control we will feel ashamed, or that we might act in ways that are different than the obedient and stifling behavior required to be socially acceptable. The more I thought about this, the more I realized how shame was so closely linked with this "killing" of passion within us.

Passion. My only remaining memories of passion in this life were identified with youth, when I knew less about society's morals and judgments about certain types of behavior. Oh, how we are all so influenced and conditioned by those around us! If we allowed ourselves to flow with our true feelings, there would be more inspiration in our world, more opportunities to create beauty and joy in our lives. After all, creativity and passion go hand in hand, and so much of our creativity has been denied because of our fears of criticism from others.

Passion has also been identified with uncontrollable emotions. And all too often, uncontrollable emotions have led to destruction and suffering for countless individuals.

"Divine Mother . . . how can we invite passion into our lives without giving in to lower emotional impulses that are bound to be destructive in some manner? I realize that being emotional is all a part of being fully human, but this passion thing frightens most people and seems to bring up so many issues for them that they don't want to face. Yet there is increasing evidence that passion is somehow related to the Divine." I surprised myself with that statement, as if new perceptions were suddenly opening to me that were not available before.

She gazed at me with those incredibly deep blue eyes that called forth a sensation which could only be described as mystical. In fact, feelings began to grow in me which were beyond what words could describe. I continued to stare into those pleasantly hypnotic eyes, wondering what would happen next.

THIRTEEN

We were enveloped in an atmosphere that seemed to buzz with electricity, appealing fragrance and unusual sound. As these exotic sensations rippled through my body, I felt as though my skin were being caressed by the finest silks and the softest of furs. Rivelets of chills moved up my spine.

I watched with wide-eyed alarm as the flowing garments that clothed Divine Mother dissolved, and her naked body was revealed to me. I felt it wrong to look upon her this way, and shut my eyes tightly, confused by the turbulent feelings and thoughts that rushed through me. I was suddenly aware that my body was naked as well, and I quickly placed my hands over the one area that I was ashamed for her to see.

This was much too embarrassing for me, and I called out, "What are you doing? This is crazy. It's indecent for me to be standing here like this with you in your bare skin and me in mine! What is all this for?" I tried to turn and run for the nearest bush, but a power stronger than my own fear held me in place.

Divine Mother laughed softly, and I felt her warm hand on my arm. "Clarion, open your eyes. Behold a miracle of creation and be glad. How can you find shame in what the beloved Creator has offered you as a magnificent vessel with which to explore the universe and experience pleasure?

Who taught you to be ashamed of those things that are wholesome and natural? Who told you that pleasure in the touching and sharing of a naked body is wrong and sinful? And why are you afraid to look upon me in my nakedness? Do you think that God will strike you down for doing so?" She laughed again, sounding sweet and melodious like shivering chimes in the wind.

Keeping my eyes shut tight, I felt unbearably awkward in this situation and wished that she would stop teasing me. "I don't want to offend you by looking at your body. After all, you are the Divine Mother."

"Oh! And what meaning has your mind made up in regards to 'Divine Mother'? It seems as though your mind has made the meaning that to be 'Divine Mother,' one must eliminate the pleasures of the body. If I am 'Mother,' then at one time did I not give birth to at least one child? And in order to give birth, did I not have a sexual encounter with a man? Will your mind make the meaning that it was sinful for me to have had a sexual encounter with a man, and even to have enjoyed it?

"Why is it that the pious in your world declare that sexual desire is sinful? Why have some of you decreed that it is sacrilegious for a man or woman to find passionate joy in giving pleasure to one another through the sharing of their bodies? Why have the clergy of your world religions insisted on admonishing that this playful activity is for procreation only?"

She squeezed my arm in earnest and pressed her hand ever so lightly against my blushing face. "I am not ashamed, Clarion. I rejoice in this body that I have chosen for the sole purpose of helping you feel more at ease with my presence. As you have learned to trust in me you have allowed me deeper into your heart. Why would the naturalness of my naked body cause you to fall into mistrust of me and mistrust of yourself? Embarrassment is simply an expression of fear that reflects lack of trust and lack of control."

"But, I'm afraid of . . . I think I'm – "

"Afraid that you may be aroused?" She giggled like a young girl engaged in a child's game. "So what if your body responds in a natural way to a sight that stimulates memories of passion and sensuousness? Have you judged this to be wrong?"

Squirming with the flood of confusion and feelings, I remembered that the conflict I was experiencing might be eased by returning to the peaceful center of the heart-mind. I became amused with the realization that I was treating this encounter like it was a dangerous threat. I wondered why I was so uneasy with all of this.

When my turbulent mind was more at ease, I opened my eyes and gazed directly into hers. Through her eyes I beheld the most innocent presence, like that of a child who only wants to explore and enjoy. Her sunlit hair wafted freely in the breeze, and I looked upon her smiling lips, softly plump with a surge of quiet burgundy. My eyes wandered slowly down the smooth skin of her neck, admiring the graceful poise of the shoulders, and lingered on the tantalizing fullness of her breasts.

A rush of heat filled my face, and I quickly looked away, ashamed of the sudden burst of desire. I knew she must know my thoughts. She reached up to touch my chin, and lifted my gaze into hers once more. She smiled an ever so inviting smile, and the warmth of acceptance filled my body and soul. I resumed my intimate study of her pleasing curves, lowering my visual journey to pause on the delicate tuft of fine hair, then followed the shapely contours of her hips, slender legs, and even the tips of her toes.

When I returned my searching eyes to her face, she was gazing with obvious appreciation at at my own body. I felt that I would blush again, but this time I was aware of an inner strength, a sense of completion, as though a missing part of me had been re-trieved from some deep and mysterious place.

Through her love and her total acceptance of my nakedness, I felt as though an abysmal yearning had been quelled, an eternal thirst quenched. As she looked into my eyes, her face glowed radiantly.

"I honor you, Clarion, and I honor this body that you have chosen for your soul's expression. I honor the spirit of you that is forever eternal and sacred." She touched the most sensitive and vulnerable areas of my body with feather-light fingertips, and a strange and wonderful power welled within me.

"Clarion," she whispered in my ear, the sensation of her breath inducing a pleasant shiver, "let the pleasurable feelings emerge and do not hold back. The power moving through you is completely natural and not to be feared. It seems a strange power to you, since you have forgotten what its presence felt like in your body. As a child, this creative and sensuous power flowed naturally and inno-cently, as it flows in all young children who have not been critically and fearfully influenced by the forgetful ones of your world.

"Children do not learn to be ashamed of themselves, nor of their bodies, until they are conditioned by the adults. Young children are very sensitive and are highly attuned to the natural, sensual world.

"As they grow up and acquire the behaviors and beliefs of adults, children are often taught to have shame about many things that are normal and appropriate in the sensuous world of nature. Eventually, most children learn to shut down their own sensuousness and become limited in their ability to experience pleasure and the deeper, more expanded joys of sexuality.

"Remember! This is the power of the divine creative

force and it *is* sensuous! Let it flood your body and soul with passion and joy!" Her words were like music, and she drew me into her embrace.

Enjoying the feel of her warm skin against mine, I gently closed my arms and drew her closer. Tears of gladness formed in my eyes as I allowed this wonderful power, this passionate force, to rush through me unimpeded.

This power was far more than mere lusty passion. It was amplified by the growing reverence and love which I felt for her. Memories of my younger years were now available as if a heavy veil of forgetfulness had been stripped away. My body, of its own volition, inhaled deeply as if for the first time, eliciting the resiliency of a more youthful era. My skin glowed with a golden red, and my body looked younger. I pulled back from her a little to examine myself more thoroughly and stretched my arms widely, as if awakening from an ancient slumber. She watched in admiration as I twisted and turned this way and that in utter enjoyment of the sudden rejuvenation of my body.

I looked at her with questioning eyes and she responded brightly, "Clarion, you have allowed yourself the pleasure of the divine creative force, the natural power, to flow unimpeded. This force is available to everyone in your world, to all in the universe. Those who reawaken to this natural vitality will rejuvenate themselves." The youthful tone of her voice was delightfully appealling.

She held her head high in regal bearing, and about her head shone a bright, golden light. "The Goddess returns to wed Her God, to reunite with Her Holy Groom through the passionate joy of divine marriage. This sacred marriage is consummated within each man and woman who chooses to create union with the feminine and masculine aspects within themselves."

When she said this, the air around us crackled and buzzed with an energy that riveted my attention on her. Waves of intense vibration flashed from my head to my toes. Something in the way she spoke generated a deep knowingness that these were words of primordial truth.

"Every man and woman who chooses to reclaim the divine spirit and passion in sexual expression and the creative passion in life's living, invites the return of the Goddess and the divine creative force that She embodies. It is She who will liberate the consciousness of humankind from the gridlock of rigid intellectualism, fear, guilt, and shame, which are rooted in the original betrayal of the divine feminine.

"Come play, Clarion! Be at peace with these natural and wholesome feelings. Experience the joy of the Goddess as She reminds you of your spiritual divinity. Be as a child again. Know yourself to be innocent once more, to be without criticism and guilt, to be natural, to be in awe of all creation, to live fully in the moment as children do so well, and to embrace the sensuousness of every experience." Her smile was radiant as she held out her hand to me. Captivated by her charming rhetoric and teasing eyes, I took her hand firmly and felt a rising of energy.

With a sweet girlish giggle, she started to run, pulling me into a rhythm that matched her own. The thick meadow grass was buoyant under our feet, making each stride an effortless spring. I laughed boldly, enthralled by the freedom I felt and by all the pleasurable bouncing sensations of my naked body. As we ran and leaped over swatches of wild flowers, I glanced at her several times, wishing to capture her child-like effervescence as a permanent memory.

We sprinted down the gentle slope of a small hill and stopped on the sunny bank of a narrow river. She looked toward a quiet pool nearby, sculpted out of the granite mounds over the centuries by torrid, rushing waters. The river waters only trickled now, into this deep hollow, creating a perfect and inviting swimming hole.

As if sharing the same idea, we sprang forward together without words, and ran hand in hand to the edge of the dry granite, catapulted ourselves into the air, and slapped the still surface of the water with the bare skin of our derrieres. The crisp chill of the water was electrifying. We squealed and shouted like boisterous children, and were fast to resort to the playful splashing of each other.

She laughed gleefully and dove beneath the surface, disappearing altogether, only to make her presence known with a firm grasp of my manhood. A bulging swell of bubbles exploded at the surface, and I was sure that her elfish laughter could be heard with each bubble that burst.

Her playful boldness was arousing, and I plunged my face into the water, only to see her blurred form quickly moving beyond my reach. The ease and power with which I could move my body through the water brought such elation that I broke to the surface in a booming guffaw. What a joy to feel so free! If only it could always be this way.

"Clarion, " she called from the shore, "It *can* always be this way! You and every man and woman are entitled to this freedom and joy as your birthright. Every man and woman must choose, however, to let go of those beliefs that stop the flow of the divine creative force, self-acceptance and love."

Climbing onto the dry bank, her wet body glistening, she scampered toward a large shrub that cast its shadow across a plush patch of meadow grass. She knelt in this spot and beckoned me to join her.

I swallowed hard at first, then felt the surge of energy in my loins. I looked downward to check on my physical status, hoping that I would not find a condition that gave clue to my excitement.

"Be grateful for the body's natural expression of enthusiasm. Let your body convince your overactive and critical mind that it is all right to play, to be child-like again and enjoy the passion of the moment." She continued with her playful coaxing, letting her warm love radiate out to me.

Wading to the edge of the pool and onto the dry granite, I stood up, daring now to fully expose my enthusiasm. I had not felt the pleasure of such bulging enthusiasm for more years than I wanted to admit, and it was glorious! All shame vanished, and with potent strides, I approached her. As I knelt down, her eyes twinkled and danced like those of a little girl witnessing her first decorated Christmas tree.

I stroked her wet hair, pulling it back gently from her cheek, and slowly advanced toward her quivering lips. As my mouth briefly touched the moist richness of hers, a swooning sensation spun through me. I drew back again to look upon her face. The shimmering jewels of beaded water were still clinging and bathed her a halo of sparkling light.

As the depth of her eyes mesmerized me, she placed her hand over my heart. "Clarion, we give to each other in the full light of the day, in full witness of our beloved creator God, in full honor of the Goddess . . . we pleasure one another in love. Let passion and desire inspire the reawakening of the spiritual essence of your body so that you may fully experience the power of the creative life force." As her eyes quickly skimmed over my body, I was aware that my heart was beating wildly. "The flush of passion that I see in you arouses in me a yearning that will only be quelled through our union. Come to me, Clarion." She kissed my lips tenderly, lingering long enough to ignite a pleasant flutter in my heart and an aching urgency in my groin.

She leaned back down to the comfort of the grassy bed, her arms stretching out beyond the top of her head; and when her hands fell upon the stems of purple wild flowers, she plucked them and pressed them reverently to her nose. Then she anchored the flowers securely behind my ears, laughing softly as she arranged them to her liking. "Clarion, you are beautiful." And she drew my face close to hers.

As our mouths touched, the sweet taste of honeyed wine consumed my senses. Soon, a divine delirium overwhelmed me, and titillating vibrations arose and fell like effervescent waves of a turbulent ocean. Her warm hands and arms caressed me lovingly and sensuously, our eyes meeting often.

I had concerns about whether I could please her, and in response to my thoughts she whispered, "Do not let your mind cast worry over this. Surrender fully to each moment of experience, and you will be in the flow of divine passion. Let your heart and soul lead you, and you will have full knowledge without concern for what is right and what is wrong." With this realization, I let go of the worry and the need to remain in control and surrendered to full passion.

How long we were entangled in a passionate dance of sensuous desire, I do not know. I only know that I was lost in the powerful sensations of ecstasy. My body, free from the fearful and critical dictates of my mind, knew all it needed to know . . . I let it take me . . . into the abysmal rifts of mystery where there seemed to be total void, nothing tangible; yet a vast, invisible presence of awesome omnipotence was everywhere. It was as though I had transcended all physical matter and entered into complete and blissful oneness with all of life.

My attention was retrieved from that fathomless nirvana to the exquisite writhing of her body entwined with mine. The soft sounds of deepening pleasure that issued from her lips were cherished music to my ears, as the crescendo of rhythm reached its climatic glory in full measure of its seeking. Breathless and well spent, we kissed each other while tears of gladness glimmered in our eyes.

We tumbled about, laughing easily, then succumbed to the silent communication of our roving hands. She rolled away from my arms to rise; and as I lay on my back in a swirl of dwindling ecstasy, she straddled my torso and sat while I rested my hands upon her smooth hips. The smiles in our eyes conveyed the contentment we shared.

"Clarion," she spoke in a low tone while studying me warmly, "this is the gift the Goddess brings. Each moment is abundant with a wealth of experience if only you will allow yourself to surrender to divine creativity in every moment. Through your willingness to surrender, to lose control, to let go of the critical judgments that keep you in fear and doubt, to become child-like again, you will open the door to the blessings of rejuvenation, passion, play, love and inspiration."

Breathing deeply, my body and soul felt more alive than ever. I knew that what she meant by surrendering to sensuousness, passion and joy in every moment was not about promiscuity; it was about trust. When we truly revere and honor the soul of another, the love that is born of that reverence and honor creates trust. Our deep trust in one another and in the divinity of all encourages us to surrender. When we surrender and become receptive, the divine creative power fills us to overflowing.

And it wasn't about abandoning our responsibilities by surrendering in every moment. It was about being sensitive and aware enough in each moment that we become available for the powerful insight or creative solution that seeks its way of expression through us. In so doing, we may live our lives more fully, enriching and enlivening

ORACLE OF CLARION

even the most mundane of daily routines.

All that I had experienced in this passionate en-
counter caused me to contemplate the fearful judgments so
many of us have around sexual conduct. Even though there
had been a history of sexual revolution, sex education in
schools, and greater public awareness of sexuality, it was
taking a long while for the new thought to take root in the
thinking and behavior throughout most of humanity.

Organized religions frowned upon easy access to
sexual material, banning these things from their own book-
stores. Although there had been movement to integrate
sexual awareness into their own educational criteria, their
approach was rather stuffy and over-intellectualized and
reflected the lack of ease with which many of the church
elders and clergy still felt about this explosive topic.

I thought about pornography and sexual abuse of
children. These perversions and distortions of sexual ex-
pression continued to exist, even though to a much lesser
degree as the public became more actively abhorrent of
these activities. But how will we finally put an end to this?

"These distortions and perversions arise from re-
pression of what is natural and wholesome." Her voice
strongly interrupted my chain of deep thought, and her
gaiety shifted into smoldering indignation.

She moved to kneel beside me, her eyes reflecting a
powerful disturbance. "When a person or society represses
the omnipotent power of the sexual nature through shame,
fear or angry judgments, this eventually erupts into unnatu-
ral and irreverent expression. Such repression causes an
overabundance of unreleased and unexpressed creative
energy, which is then made toxic by an overload of fearful
and shameful input into the human psyche.

"Observe the analogy of enormous public garbage
pits, piled high with layer upon layer of spoiled rubbish that
puts forth disgusting, noxious fumes. No matter how

many tons of earth you heap upon it to cover it up, to make it look more attractive, and to stop the smell, this rubbish under pressure encourages the buildup of poisonous gas. Eventually, the laws of nature will always have their way. Seeking to relieve the pressure, the disgusting fumes find a way to the surface to offend again. So it is with the outcome of repression.

"The unhealthy cultural judgments that are rooted in fear and anger teach those in your world to repress natural sexual expression with layer upon layer of guilt, denial, and shame. These are often amplified by threats of punishment in some form or other in an attempt to control the situation. This approach only succeeds in creating more pressure, which eventually erupts into your society in the form of uneasiness with sex, unhealthy sexual attitudes, perversions and sexual violations. That is why pornography and sexual abuse of children abound in those societies that are the most sexually repressed.

"One who tries to satisfy his yearning for closeness and natural sexual union through the observance of pornography very often starves himself of the wholesome and joyful flow of sexual passion. Such a person becomes riddled with guilt or shame at the mere thought of a sexual fantasy, let alone a live sexual encounter with a real person. He or she then finds it difficult to create a deeply meaningful, intimate and mature relationship with another, since a healthy and loving relationship with the personal self has not yet been achieved."

Across her face a shroud of foreboding spread, and I became uneasy as a raging, quaking fire burned in her eyes. "And those confused souls who resort to invading the sanctity of a child's body to satisfy their need for closeness or sexual expression will sever themselves from the divine, and *if they persist* with this behavior, *there is no grace for them!*"

My body trembled in full knowingness that child abuse was one of the most horrid of all violations that could occur, and that those who participated in such activities would in some way suffer horrible retribution.

She continued, "They seek to find some manner of love and contentment in their lives, yet until they discover the everpresent power of God and Goddess within, they will never find what they search for outside of themselves." The fire in her eyes subsided, giving way to compassion and sadness, a reflection of her concern for the darker side of human nature.

She looked at me, her eyes soft and sparkling once more. Smiling brightly, she bent over to kiss me, and I reached for her and pulled her close. As I held her, I became aware of a flood of feelings stirring inside me. I was so very grateful for her and all that she had shown me.

Her power as Divine Mother was unquestionable; she was awesome and sometimes even frightening. Yet here she lay in my arms, tender and inviting. She had surrendered herself completely to me, to our shared experience, and I was in total bliss. I had gone through every conceivable feeling and emotion during my time with her, in all that I encountered.

If she was the embodiment of the Goddess, then all that has transpired down through the ages of religious dogma was all about squelching the fires of desire within humanity. Overthrowing the Goddess was all about repressing our natural creative passion, our link to the divine!

In fear of our emotions and fear of losing control, we have repressed ourselves to the point of sterility; we are sterile in the realms of creativity, passion and sexual intimacy. So many of us are dried up inside for lack of inspiration, and we are uninspired because we have closed ourselves off from the Goddess. Among many other things,

She represents the richness and moistness of fertility that gives rise to creation, creative imagination and the ability to conceive and put forth our ideas, visions and dreams, to give them birth and to share them with the world.

Without the Goddess, we have become quite lifeless in our cultures, lacking depth, enthusiasm and fulfillment in our personal lives. We live mostly in our heads, our intellects, and we try to reason ourselves through all of life situations. We have lost touch with our feelings. We have lost passion. How will we ever change these things within ourselves?

She said that the Goddess comes to wed her God and that this will occur within every man and woman who invites inspiration, love, passion, play, creativity, peace, and a child-like attitude toward life experience. Lest we become like children, we cannot inherit the kingdom of God . . . the phrase in the Bible went something like that. Pondering these ideas was wonderfully electrifying, and I knew them to be truths for all of us in the world.

Raising her body to stretch across mine, head to toe, she looked deeply into my eyes and came close to kiss me. And as her sweet mouth pressed against mine, something extraordinary happened. My eyes closed in contented reverie and she melted into me, all of her. I lay there, giving way to complete seduction, enraptured with this marvelous and mysterious feeling. She and I became one.

The sensation was profoundly moving, as wave upon wave of soothing peace and infinite knowingness settled into the deepest part of my being. Boundless and free, my consciousness expanded well beyond the limits of my memory. I could not hold onto the experience with my mind, for there was no longer any thought nor word that could contain the meaning of this experience. I was everything, and everything was me. I was God, I was Goddess, and the exhilaration was astounding. I was not sure of anything anymore. No meaning of worldly description could be applied. Eternal bliss and infinite oneness were mine. This was divine ecstasy!

I became one with the universe and knew myself to be whole and complete. Full of joy, I laughed exuberantly, and the echo of my cosmic cheer reverberated throughout creation. I was free to go anywhere and to do anything. The power moved like a cosmic tidal wave, omnipresent and magnificent, and I rode upon it effortlessly.

The stars and planets were spectacular points of dancing light, spinning amidst the gaseous clouds of shimmering nebulae and the opulent, velvet darkness of deep space. I gloried in it, reveled in it. I longed to be everywhere, to be all places at once, to experience everything. With this powerful desire, I felt myself explode in a mighty burst that rocked my soul profoundly, and yet the sensation was so fantastic, so incredibly ecstatic that I was happy beyond comprehension. It was as if numberless facets of myself went out into all of the universe, like the rays of a brilliant sun, which casts its brightness upon all things.

As I watched creation erupt with the excitement and extravaganza of vibrant life everywhere, my attention was sharply drawn to one corner of the universe. This chasm of space beckoned me, pulled me; and I found myself speeding through the void, the flash of passing stars and planets a mere blur. Coming to an abrupt halt, I was weightless and poised high above an illuminated planet that shone like a polished pearl.

The iridescent and inspiring beauty of this planet was breathtaking, and I studied the golden brown masses of land and the glimmering aquamarine waters. The vibration of this cosmic oasis thundered through my being with the emergence of a feeling that could only be described as the most powerful love. I wanted to caress and nurture this entire planet. Tears came, and I yearned to reach out and touch all of it, to merge with every life form that lived there.

With that thought, it was as if I became one with the wind, the air, and the waters. I split exponentially, trillions of times, into infinitesimal particles of light, spreading in limitless form everywhere, into all the living kingdoms that claimed this globe as home.

Penetrating every conceivable life form, from the smallest of groping invertebrates to the largest of ocean creatures, from the tiniest of delicate mosses to the enormity of mountain ranges, I pressed on to observe and mingle with all of life.

I watched life evolve and was united with it. Wherever I focused my attention, there I appeared in essence. Merging with the cells of a young body, through the eyes of a child I beheld the grandeur of creation, and paused in that moment to relish the innocent interpretation of life.

Rapidly moving on, I next became one with the life expression of a grown man struggling with life challenges and reaping the rewards of perserverance.

Then I was one with a woman straining with the pangs of giving birth, crying out in agony, soon crying in joy as a tiny, whimpering form nestled in her nurturing arms.

Becoming one with a dying elder, I felt the last moments of life ebb away, leaving behind the empty husk of a body to be placed in a dark casket. It was buried deep in the ground, only to dribble away into the decay of life, to recycle itself and rise to become a vital part of life again.

Was this the experience of many lifetimes? Was this a passing of eons? I had no recollection nor sense of aging. All I knew was this lavish consummation with all of life, and I understood myself to be an intimate, sensuous part of every living thing that occupied the land or the seas. The flames of even deeper love and compassion were ignited, and I returned to hover over the planet once more, in full knowledge and recognition that this was my home, my beloved Earth!

I knew of the Earth in a different way now, and longed for a deepening kinship with her and with my fellow human beings. Gazing in wonder at the world, I thought about the people, each person in the process of living life and experiencing personal life lessons. Each person was different, each was unique, and each person had a purpose, a specific function on the planet. No one could act in the world without impacting someone or something else. We were all interconnected. We were all, quite literally, one family, a global family. I saw humanity clearly as one people sharing the same home in space. It was an awesome realization, and my heart beat with great fervor in this miraculous moment.

It no longer mattered that some people were of different colors or beliefs. It no longer mattered that there were separate nations and states. It no longer mattered that some were weak and some were strong, that some were wealthy and some were poor, that some were at war and others at peace. It was as if all of humanity merged into one colossal entity in the shared throes of challenging life situations, having all the various moods and expressions of the troubled pubescent phase of a young adolescent.

I closed my eyes, lost in the feeling of oneness and appreciation for all of life. My thoughts began to take form around those I had come to love the most. Images of Mathias flashed through my mind, and I missed him. His delightful self had won a place in my heart, and I wondered if I would ever see him again. Lola had captivated me with her warmth, charm, and attractiveness. I had wanted to spend more time with her, to get to know her. Murphy, dear Murphy, my closest friend and devoted aide. How was he? And how goes the Presidency? The Presidency! I *am* the President!

FOURTEEN

A torrent of memories jolted me, and every cell, every molecule buzzed and quaked. Where had I been? What had I been doing all this time? And my daughter, my lovely daughter, what has happened to her after all these days . . . weeks . . . years? How long . . . ?

My heart raced, while I fought furiously to open my eyes. Streams of vicious, white energy ripped through me. It felt as though I was careening recklessly on some crazy bobsled ride, shooting down an ominous mountain precipice. Out of control and falling fast, I groped for something to hang onto, anything. There was only a mighty wind and a deafening sound. I called out in desperation and heard a familiar whisper, coming from somewhere inside of me.

"Clarion! Remember . . . the peace and freedom from fear that you seek is forever in the heart-mind!"

It was Divine Mother, speaking to me from deep within! I breathed a long sigh of relief and reminded myself of that peaceful place inside me.

I imagined once more the beautiful, peaceful meadow, the serene vistas and quietly gurgling waters. Breathing easily and achieving a deeper sense of calm, I felt the turbulent energy subside. Floating now, I felt at ease while the growing calmness reassured me and brought a comforting smile to my face.

As I gradually drifted downward, feeling relaxed and trusting, I was able to open my eyes and to see a blurry light approaching. I was high in the clouds, surrounded by wisps of silverwhite and a light in the distance, which grew larger and brighter.

As the light came close, it pulsated with glistening, etheric membranes that stretched widely to either side. I realized that these were wings! The huge spread of the gracefully undulating wings was dazzling. I was spellbound as this creature of light took on the appearance of a young person, a person who had wings.

Awestruck by the brilliance of this being, I felt my heart vibrate strongly in response to a power that was loving, wise and wonderful. The near blinding radiance of this being made it difficult to make out the details of the face. Yet, as it came nearer, there was something familiar about the features. All at once, I knew who it was.

"Mathias! Is that you?" I blurted out in amazement. He smiled that same sweet, innocent smile of his.

"You look like . . . like an angel!"

"I *am* an angel. I always have been. I just lost my wings for a while, that's all." He spoke matter-of-factly, as if I understood what he was talking about.

"What do you mean? You had a physical body like mine. You lived other lives. You were a little boy and you _ " I stopped, remembering that any attempt to make sense of anything involving Mathias was usually . . . well, usually senseless.

"I just finished my last earth life as a human being," Mathias said, radiant with a new glow that was vibrantly alive and translucent. "All my life lessons are done. I don't have to be born in a physical body ever again unless I really want to. My very last mission on earth was to guide you to Divine Mother. I was worried at first that you weren't going to go along with the plan, and that there would be a long delay before I could get my wings back."

He hovered effortlessly on the magical buoyancy of wings that kept a slow and powerful rhythm as he added,

"When we first met in the hospital, you only saw me in the body that I manifested for the assignment. I had already died from an accident a few months before. It was hard to watch my parents grieving over my death because they didn't know that I was safe in spirit. I've been visiting them in their dreams and letting them know that I'm okay. Little by little, as they share their dreams with each other, they are beginning to understand that I was ready to return to Angelhood. My last physical life was only meant to be a short one because my earth lessons were ending and I was up for graduation.

"The part I played in helping you wake up to a greater truth was my very last lesson, my last assignment, and I made it. So thank you, Clarion! Thank you for trusting me and letting me guide you to Divine Mother. I am so happy!" The radiance of Mathias glittered brightly, and his musical laughter echoed among the clouds.

"Remember, Clarion," he instructed, "none of this is supposed to make any sense to your mind. Never try to make sense of a miracle."

Still floating through billows of white, I was dumbfounded with this new awareness about him. But then, the whole chain of events from the hospital to this moment was so incredible that nothing was too weird anymore. Nothing made any sense to my rational mind, and finally I felt all right with that.

"Clarion," Mathias became a little serious as he spoke. "It's time for you to return home and resume your life, but you will never be the same. Your life and the world will look much different, and you will make great changes in the world." As he said this, he looked into my eyes with such loving admiration that I became tearful, and knew that I would miss him terribly.

"Hold in your heart the images of those you love; hold on to your new awareness of the beauty and magnificence of the earth and all the people who share this planet. And be happy! I will always be with you as your guardian angel."

His last sentence took me by surprise, and I was ecstatic. Every fiber of my being delighted with this revelation. Mathias . . . my guardian angel! What a wild idea.

As I turned my thoughts to those I loved, and to the promising possibilities of a new earth in the making and a new humanity rising, I was elated.

I began to fall again, only this time it was without fear. Mathias took his place right beside me, firmly holding my arm as if to ensure that I would not fall too fast. Not one sliver of sky or land could be seen through the thickness of the clouds. I did not know where I was headed. As we journeyed downward, he reminded me often to keep my attention on the heart-mind.

My eyes closed heavily as if invaded with a deep sleep, and I struggled to keep awake. Mathias still held on to me, and oddly enough I felt safe. As I gradually lost consciousness, a myriad of images exploded across my inner vision in kaleidoscopic procession, offering a fantastic review of all my experiences with Mathias and Divine Mother.

The flashing of images quickened, smashing violently and disintegrating one into the other until an enormous collage of cosmic proportions circled slowly like a colossal whirlpool before me. Everything blended into one vast and rumbling rotating form.

I fell into the massive spiral, and as my awareness came to rest in its very center, I remembered the words of Divine Mother, " . . . to be at peace with one's self is like being in the eye of the hurricane." And I was here, in the center of it all, calm and at peace, while all about me was chaos and turbulence.

Through the clarity that this peace allowed, I became one with every event in a twinkling of an eye. I was aware of every feeling and thought, every decision and choice, every transformative experience that occurred during my amazing journey. A deep sense of satisfaction and a new understanding were now integral parts of my being, and the empowerment I felt was awesome. I was grateful beyond words.

As I reveled in the glory of this new understanding, the massive spiral quietly disappeared, dissolving into a peaceful nothingness. As I slipped deeper into the void, a sweet, comforting darkness enveloped me. I drifted serenely, like a newborn child cuddled safely in the arms of its mother.

Unusual sounds gained my attention. Annoyed with the interruption, I reluctantly followed them, curious to discover who or what would dare to disturb my bliss. I seemed unable to open my eyes, so I relied on my ears to find the origin of these strange noises.

At first, I became aware of resting on something solid; and as I cautiously moved my fingers and hands to explore, I felt what seemed like a bed. I finally managed to open my eyes, but the surroundings were still a blur, making it difficult to determine where I was.

The strange sounds continued to buzz and click somewhere over my head. As my vision cleared, I noticed that there were white curtains all around me, and I could see the fuzzy shapes of people standing at the foot of the bed. I blinked several times, and the shapes came into focus. The first that I could distinguish among them was Murphy. Murphy! How wonderful to see him again!

"Murphy!" My voice cracked and rasped dryly. "I've . . . just had . . . the most . . . incredible . . . experience . . ." The words came like a whisper as I strained to speak.

"President Agate!" Murphy rushed to my side, taking my hand and squeezing firmly. "Don't speak now, just rest. You've had quite a bit of trauma. Let the Doctor take care of you."

I looked to the other side of the bed and remembered the pensive man in white and the petite nurse standing next to him. He was holding my wrist, as doctors seem to want to do, and I managed a feeble grin. A flood of memories rushed into my mind, and I recalled the assassination attempt. I remembered being shot, and then became concerned about the injuries.

"Murphy, will my voice be saved? How bad are my injuries?" My words were gaining strength rapidly as full consciousness returned.

"You were only grazed on the neck, sir. The impact knocked you unconscious. We were all deeply shocked and worried to death for you. The whole nation is awaiting news of your recovery, and your daughter is flying in at this very moment." Murphy's voice wavered from his usual confident manner as he added, "We don't know how you escaped more severe injury. Frankly, we're all quite baffled with the minor damage . . . it should have been much worse. Can you explain, Doctor?"

The doctor hesitated, clearing his throat several times before he spoke. "We were certain that the tissue and bone damage was severe enough to warrant surgery. However, once the wound was cleaned, it was simply a matter of a few stitches. In all honesty, Mr. President, I'm not sure what happened. I've never seen anything like it before. One moment the damage was obviously serious enough to be life threatening, and the next moment it was as if a miracle occurred. It's the damnedest thing I've ever seen in all my years of practice."

The room became quiet, as if an air of reverence descended on everyone. Somewhere inside me a quiet voice whispered, "Never try to make sense of a miracle."

I recalled Divine Mother's healing presence, which seemed more like a dream now, as I lay once more in the hospital bed. Did it all really happen?

"Murphy? How long have I been here? What time is it?"

"You've been here since this morning, sir. It's early evening, and I'm afraid you've missed dinner." Murphy joked, but his deep concern was obvious. "Don't worry, Mr. President, if you're hungry, the hospital kitchen staff is on call for your special order. Anything you desire, sir. That is, if your desire meets with the Doctor's approval."

Scarcely hearing his words, I was stunned to learn that my incredible adventure occurred in less than a day! I had only been in the hospital since this morning? How can that be? So much happened! What about the car trip to the mountains? What about that arduous climb up the granite wall, and the long hike to the meadow? What about all those past-life experiences? And Mathias? Divine Mother? The cosmic journey through space and that . . .

I grew dizzy with confusion and felt the blood drain from my face. It must have been quite noticeable, for the doctor instantly ordered everyone out of the room. He and the nurse remained, their fading forms the last image I saw before passing out.

Surrounded by darkness, I called out for help, only to hear a familiar voice directly behind me: "I'm still here, Clarion. I haven't gone anywhere. I'll always be here." Mathias, flapping his glorious wings, was hovering at eye level.

"Mathias! I'm so glad to see you. But I'm so confused . . ." I didn't know how to convey my dilemma.

"It all happened, Clarion . . . really! I'm here, and Divine Mother is always with you. She's a part of you now, and a part of all those who invite the Goddess into their

sleep?" Murphy quipped brightly as he assisted the nurse
in preparing me for breakfast. "You gave us a scare last
night. But the Doctor assured me that fainting often ac-
companies such conditions."

"It's morning?" I looked to the window as an atten-
dant gently pushed her way through the flank of security
guards. When she pulled up the blinds, I could see a few
windblown clouds drifting across the early dawn colors of
pink and blue. Memories of the sky over the meadow
flooded back to my mind.

"President Agate, your daughter arrived late last
night. Once it was clear that you were fine and resting
well, rather than disturb you, she went quickly to a nearby
hotel. She was tired and very concerned about you, but felt
much better with the news of your improvement. Relatives
and friends are with her, as well as enough security personel,
so she is in good hands, sir." Murphy went about the room
briskly, examining everything to make sure that all was in
order for my comfort. "By the way, I have something to
give to you from a young admirer."

As he turned to walk out the door, I called out to

him. "Murphy, " I gestured him to come to my side. As he leaned close to my face, I whispered, "call me Clarion when we're not in the presence of the White House staff or the public, will you?"

The astonishment on Murphy's face was comical, his eyes wide with disbelief, and I had to cover my mouth to keep from laughing.

"Oh, sir, I couldn't possibly . . . " he blurted out while his eyes darted uneasily about the room.

"Please! It would give me great pleasure. You've been a good friend, Murphy." I looked at him and sent all the love I could.

His eyes glistened and his cheeks flushed as he responded with the biggest smile I'd ever seen on his face. "Very well, sir . . . I mean . . . Clarion, sir . . . I mean . . . well . . . it will take some getting used to. Thank you, sir . . . uh . . . Clarion. I'll be right back with that little something from the young admirer."

As he hurried out the door, I muffled a soft chuckle as the affection I felt for Murphy warmed my heart. He returned with a small white box and a stack of opened telegrams in his hands.

"There is a growing crowd of concerned folks outside of the hospital, sir . . . Clarion. Many of them have delivered beautiful bouquets of flowers which we have placed in another room. Of course, we cannot bring the flowers in to your room — doctor's orders, you know. However, here are some telegrams, sent by well-wishers from all over the world, that might cheer you. And in this little box is a rather special item." Murphy handed me the box. It had already been opened and its contents thoroughly examined, I knew, for security reasons.

I lifted the lid, and peeled back the wrapping to find the gold Mother Mary lapel pin! The startled expression on my face alarmed Murphy, and he moved in close.

"Is it *that* special, sir? . . . Clarion?" He examined the pin with his piercing gaze. "A very charming little boy in the crowd outside handed it to one of the security guards. He was quite insistent that you receive it. Tell me, please, what is it?"

Unable to speak, I lifted the pin out of the box and turned it around to read the inscription. "What!" My outburst caused Murphy to fidget nervously.

"You've got me bursting with curiosity! Can you at least tell me if you are all right?" Murphy's anxiety was further fueled by my speechlessness; so I read the engraved line on the back of the lapel pin: "Blessed, loved, and protected art thou, Clarion, all the days of your life . . . and never try to make sense of a miracle." How did that last line get there? I realized that this was the evidence Mathias told me to look for – the proof that it all really happened!

I grinned broadly, while the face of Murphy deepened with bewilderment. I reached up and patted him reassuringly on the shoulder, "I'll tell you all about it later, Murphy. Don't worry, I'm doing just fine. In fact, I'm feeling pretty damned marvelous." I attached the lapel pin to my hospital robe and sat up in bed with a burst of new strength and vigor.

"Now. . . tell me about the person who tried to assassinate me? How is this matter being handled?" The power in my voice gained a new demeanor from Murphy as he straightened his shoulders, puffed out his chest, and stood more erect.

"He is being held in custody under maximum security, sir." Murphy's voice raised to an angry pitch as he clenched his fists. With a forward thrust of his jaw added, "He has been in interrogation since yesterday. We will get to the bottom of this, even if we have to torture the miserable – "

"What was his childhood like?" I demanded.

Murphy, appearing stunned, stared at me. "His childhood, sir? I'm afraid I don't know what you mean. All that we know about him so far is — "

"I mean exactly what I said!" Losing patience, I pounded on the bed railing. "What was his childhood like? Has anyone tried to understand why he is the way he is? Something terrible must have happened to him while he was growing up. Perhaps he was severely abused as a child. Maybe he feels lonely, useless, and unloved."

"W‾well . . . sir . . ." Murphy stuttered in bewilderment. " . . . all we were able to find out at this time is that he is from an impoverished background, a high school drop out, a radical, and a ‾ "

"Get him into the rehabilitation program right away!" I commanded.

"What rehabilitation program?"

"The program that educates the disadvantaged ones of the world, and helps them to recognize that they are valuable and precious, that they are loved and needed!" Passionate inspiration flooded through me like an electrical charge. Again I pounded the bed railing with my fist. My words sharply punctuated the air, and drew a crowd of nurses and security personnel to the open doorway.

The doctor's attempt to calm me was futile, and I raged on. "When the troubled people of this world understand that they are unique and special . . . when they discover that they are worthy of love and respect, no one will ever harm another person again! Crime will end. War will be non-existent. When people have love, honor, and respect for themselves, it's natural for them to love, honor, and respect other fellow human beings. When people are out of touch with what is sacred within themselves, it's more difficult for them to recognize and respect what is sacred in another. So get him into that program!"

Murphy stood motionless, looking at me as though I had lost all sense. After a moment of silence, he spoke slowly, "Sir, what you speak of has great merit, and I acknowledge the importance of such things; however, we have no such program."

"What!" I bellowed. "Then dammit, we'll create one! Send for my secretary! Get me access to all the necessary documentation and information I need we're going to generate a piece of legislation that will blow those rigid minds in Congress. I don't care how long it takes to do it or what old conservative codgers I'll have to wrangle with to get it done! I will persevere until it passes; and when we're finished with that, I have other social improvement programs to propose.

"We need to clean up this planet and heal the hearts of humanity. We all have to do our part to encourage the less fortunate of our world. We must do it to the best of our ability, in whatever manner we can, no matter how small or large our individual contribution is.

"We are Americans! We continue to set the trend for change in the world. All nations look upon us as the model for their own development and progress. We will continue to provide that model! The model of progress that we will set is that of the human potential movement. We will shift the bulk of our national spending from military defense to healthy human development and relationships. It will take time, patience, and diligence. Old belief systems, doubts and fears will have to be broken through. But we *will* do it, and we will do it with compassion, perserverance, courage, and understanding!"

Murphy's face lit up gloriously with the gaping smile of a surprised, young school boy, and the small crowd of hospital personnel and security guards broke into applause. Mustering regal Presidential bearing, I roared,

"Well! Don't you all have important work to do?" With that, everyone scattered to their stations, leaving Murphy, the doctor, and the petite nurse at my bedside.

"I'm so delighted that you are your old self again, sir — beyond delighted, in fact. I'll get on the project immediately, sir. I'll have pertinent information coming in for you right away." Murphy, excited by the challenge of this new endeavor, darted toward the door.

He stopped and thought for a moment, then said softly, "Actually, Clarion, I believe you are better than your old self. I'm not quite sure what has come over you, but I am inspired by your enthusiastic spirit." We shared a long gaze of mutual affection, and he tuned and left the room. I sighed deeply, feeling the pleasant warmth of inspiration in my heart.

I touched the Mother Mary lapel pin with renewed awe, realizing that it represented the power of the Goddess. The Goddess was returning . . . I knew it was true . . . for I felt it in my heart and in my soul. It meant the return of compassion, understanding, and service to one another. It meant that love had a new meaning: it could be powerful and tough as well as soft and sweet. The return of the Goddess meant that men and women of all nations must generate new, more creative perspectives about each other. Humankind must be willing to let go of the resentments of the past. People must take responsibility for those things they have created in their own lives and stop blaming each other for their unhappy conditions. There are no victims, and never have been.

The return of the Goddess meant that we are to move into a deeper relationship with ourselves, and to develop the heart-mind awareness within each of us.

The Goddess returning is about rekindling our passions for creativity, play and personal fulfillment. It is all about the revitalizing of life itself; about honoring and respecting each other, the earth, and all living things.

There was much work ahead for me, many visions and plans to share with my administration, the American people, and the world at large. It would be an enormous challenge. Many would resist my plans and would perceive the vision as "mission impossible," or mere fantasy. Some might even regard the vision as a threat to the Old Order.

Yet, the excitement of the possibilities and potentials motivated and inspired me. I knew that the power of the Goddess, the creative life force, was present and that it would be up to me to initiate and direct this force into mainstream America in meaningful and peaceful ways.

I thought of the long haul ahead, but I was invigorated. It was a challenge that I gladly accepted. The power of Divine Mother and all the many facets of her being burned radiantly within my soul, and I knew that her presence and wisdom would always guide me.

I lay back and closed my eyes, and memories of my fabulous journey flitted across my inner vision. Envisioning our peaceful and pearlescent world spinning in space, I gave thanks to Gaia, the spirit of our planet.

All at once, the face of Lola appeared vividly, those youthful, twinkling eyes beckoning. Her extraordinary vitality and grace had made a lasting impression on me. She was sensitive yet powerful and possessed insightful wisdom that would be most welcome on this daring venture to transform the challenging conditions of humanity.

The more I thought of her, the more difficult it became not to think about her, and the more radiant her face became to my inner vision. Somehow I knew without a doubt that she would gladly accept an invitation to the White House. And somehow I knew that she would contribute something quite important.

I began to realize that this task of reformation looming before me needed far more than my own male energy and power. I needed a strong female presence as well, in order to draw in and integrate the returning Goddess consciousness. I was beginning to see that in partnership with each other we might be able to accomplish what would be impossible to do alone. What form such a partnership might take remained a mystery . . . but I looked forward to exploring the possibilities with Lola when she arrived.

As I continued to contemplate the days ahead, a pleasant feeling arose within me. Gentle shivers went up my spine and a sly grin warmed my face, as I imagined a bright and spirited future soon to come.

About the Author

After a profound spiritual awakening in 1977, Paula Peterson pursued an intense spiritual path, and relinquished an eleven year career in Motion Picture Technologies and withdrawing from the raising and training of show-quality Arabian horses. Thereafter, she experienced several years of life-altering initiations and inspiring messages from otherworldly visitors. Paula is now on the heart-path and "on purpose" as an intuitive consultant, public speaker, author and personal and spiritual growth facilitator. Since 1989, she continues to be a featured guest on TV and radio talk shows. Her lecture tours in Japan brought recognition of her work, airing nationally on major network television. Now single and deeply dedicated to her life work, she presently resides in Northern California, where she has a private practice and spiritual learning center.

About the Publisher

Jerry Drobesh spent his adult years as a college student, Air Force officer, pilot, and built, owned, and operated a large child care center and elementary school. Along the way, he was blessed with three beautiful children and a wife who have taught him the true meaning of life-love. He experienced a spiritual awakening in 1984 with the assistance of his recently deceased sister, Karyl. Jerry met Paula in 1990 and began a wild adventure that is still expanding his awareness of God's Plan. He has been guided to establish a book publishing business, through the inspiration of a rainbow and the mystery of the pyramid.

ORDER FORM

Postal Orders: RAINBOW PYRAMID PUBLISHERS
P.O. Box 2437
Fair Oaks, CA   95628 USA

Phone & FAX Orders: 916-363-3100

On-line/E-Mail: rainbow@interx.com

Please send the *The Oracle of Clarion* to:

Name: _____

Address: _____

City: _____ **State:** _____ **Zip:** _____

Telephone: (___) _____

Shipping and Sales tax:

Please add $2.50 for books shipped to California addresses. Add 75 cents
for each addition book in same order.
(Surface shipping may take three to four weeks)
Air Mail: $3.50 per book

Payment:
☐ Cheque
☐ Money Order

Comments:

_____

_____

_____

ORDER FORM

Postal Orders: RAINBOW PYRAMID PUBLISHERS
P.O. Box 2437
Fair Oaks, CA   95628   USA

Phone & FAX Orders: 916-363-3100

On-line/E-Mail: rainbow@interx.com

Please send the *The Oracle of Clarion* to:

Name: _____

Address: _____

City: _____   **State:** _____   **Zip:** _____

Telephone: (   ) _____

Shipping and Sales tax:
Please add $2.50 for books shipped to California addresses. Add 75 cents
for each addition book in same order.
(Surface shipping may take three to four weeks)
Air Mail: $3.50 per book

Payment:
☐ Cheque
☐ Money Order

Comments:
_____

_____

_____